Foot
Fortu

Football Fortunes

by
W.A.Hunter

First Published in Great Britain
in 1996 by ....

Oldcastle Books
18 Coleswood Road
Harpenden, Herts. AL5 1EQ

A catalogue record of this book is available from
the British Library

ISBN 1-874061-69-6 Football Fortunes

Football Fortunes makes vital reading for those interested in soccer results forecasting, the football pools, or fixed-odds betting.

Comprehensive advice is provided for both novice and experienced better. Beginning with the fundamentals of results prediction and the laws of probability and odds, there then follow detailed explanations of forecasting systems and staking strategies.

To improve *your* fortunes, there are many original and innovative entries for the football pools and bookmaker's coupons. The reader will also gain some insight into the history of football betting on pools and fixed-odds.

For the computer user there are descriptions of forecasting software and examples of program code, although a knowledge of computing is not a prerequisite to a full understanding and enjoyment of this book.

All in all, *Football Fortunes* is brim-full of betting statistics, tips and practical examples.

The subject has rarely, if ever, been so extensively covered.

The Football Yearbook

This software, to which you will find several references in *Football Fortunes*, takes the form of a computerised football annual for Personal Computers using *Microsoft™* Windows.

The program comes with tables and results for the major English and Scottish leagues over the last ten seasons. The minor leagues, commonly found on football coupons, are also included.

There are several forecasting methods, with full access to predictive formulae and parameters. There are facilities for the user to input results, and update league tables for the current season.

The program provides comprehensive statistical analyses of results, tables and forecasts.

The graphics, printing, clipboard and mouse operations, are those you would associate with top quality *Windows* software.

Current fixture lists can be obtained at a small extra cost, and, if required, a regular update service can be provided using e-mail. For an additional charge it is possible to supply the soccer enthusiast with results and tables for the complete 20th century ! Details upon registration.

To readers of *Football Fortunes* the '*Yearbook*' is priced at £17.00 (including post, packing, etc). Payment is by cheque, postal order, or credit card. The *Yearbook* is supplied with full results and tables (since 1987) up to the date of despatch.

Forth Dimension,
28 Macbeth Road,
Dunfermline, Fife. KY11 4EG

Tel. or Fax : 01383 721729
E-mail : Soccerslot@aol.com
http://users.aol.com/soccerslot/forthdim.html

Available from September 1996.
Your enquiries are most welcome.

GAMBLING
SOFTWARE
USERS
GROUP

Why not join this group and benefit from the pooled expertise of its many members ?

The benefits of membership are as follows .....

1. A tri-annual newsletter telling you what is new and helpful in the world of computer gambling, including accounts by the membership of triumph (or disaster !).

2. Listings of commercial software.

3. Supply, at minimum cost, of any software available as shareware, or in the public domain.

4. A welcome package which includes a small PC compatible program on disk for you to try out.

5. If a breakthrough is achieved by any member you will be notified !

The cost of annual membership is £9.00, designed purely to defray the costs of the newsletter and operating the group.

Padraig Kirby

GAMBLING SOFTWARE
USERS GROUP *(Fortunes)*
THE RETREAT
13 HOLLY ROAD
NORTHAMPTON   NN1 4QL

Telephone : 01604 24744

Football Fortunes

5/4	Derby	9/4	Nottm.For.	7/4
8/13	Southend	12/5	West Brom	4/1
4/7	Wolves	12/5	Watford	9/2
3/1	Barnet	9/4	Port Vale	4/5
6/5	Wigan	9/4	Torquay	15/8
1/2	Kettering	12/5	Gateshead	5/1
		9/4	Rangers	5/6
		12/5	Hearts	11/2
		9/4	Stirling	5/4
			Forfar	7/4

1 2 3 4 5 6 7 8 9 10 11 12 13 14 15 16 17 18 19 20

Results Forecasting Gambling and Computing

Contents of Football Fortunes

x

Introducing Football Fortunes

To gamble or to 'game' was, according to Dr. Johnson's *Dictionary of the English Language* (1755), 'to play wantonly or extravagantly for money'. This censorious definition sums up the prevailing attitude to gambling over centuries, for there have been few occasions when Joe Punter has not had to contend with government sanctions or interference from the church.

The Victorian moralists believed that the activities of drink, sex and gambling threatened the values of hard work, thrift and self-denial. Too much gambling was indicative of a something for nothing attitude. Strangely enough, while gambling has been seen to endanger the morals of the poor, it has invariably been regarded as an acceptable pastime for the rich. The direct consequence of these double standards has been the introduction of many ill-conceived laws. It may surprise you, for example, that High Street bookmaking became legal only in 1961.

Over many years the working class punter has registered disapproval of all restrictive gambling laws by ignoring them, and continued to bet regardless of state and church intervention.

Fortunately, in current times a more enlightened attitude exists, and there is little serious opposition to gambling. Indeed, in 1994, with the advent of the UK lottery, and its phenomenal success, gaming activities have gained renewed impetus. Gambling is now a national pastime.

Today the Government continues to liberalise its policy towards football pools and betting shops, and it is hoped that these legislative changes will make football betting more attractive. However this will only happen if the pools companies and bookmakers have the foresight to meet the challenge. Deservedly or not, football gambling, particularly in the High Street, retains a seedy image and is still perceived by many to be the preserve of the ne'er-do-well or Andy Capp-style character. To appeal to a wider audience, it would seem prudent to introduce new, fairer and more adventurous betting options; while the response to the competition of the lottery should not be to take the easy solution of shaving more percentage points off the return to the punter. Undoubtedly the lottery has cost the pools industry clients and money. However, with further Government deregulation in the pipeline, and the growing realisation that the lottery is an appalling gamble, there is every chance that the decline will be reversed.

.... the greater the effort the 'luckier' you become !

Gambling and sport are inseparable, and the idea of football betting, or at least a public competition for prizes, began earnestly in the sporting press, and with bookmakers, in the 1880s and 1890s. This ultimately led, in the 1920s, to the introduction of the football 'pools'.

Contrary to popular belief, the sports better tends not to bet on 'anything that moves', but gambles on games such as soccer for which there exists a well-established attraction. It is likely that as long as the sport of football remains popular so too will football betting.

The growth in sports betting has been accompanied by the rise of the 'tipster', who purports to introduce the influence of 'skill and knowledge' to the forecasting process.... although he is by no means a modern phenomenon. One of the earliest records relates to a W.J.Duckworth of Lancaster who, in 1879, attempted to make his fortune by selling a flysheet entitled *'The Incomparable Football Forecasting System'*.

Over the 20th century the number of forecasting experts rose rapidly, particularly from the 1930s, when the football pools really took off. In 1951, Harry Bone, a famous professional forecaster of his time, stated (*not altogether surprisingly considering his occupation*) that the efforts made, and options available to predict football results, put the pools beyond the status of a *mere* lottery.

By the way, if you have a specific interest in the *history* of sports betting in Britain, *'A Bit of a Flutter'* by Mark Clapson, is highly recommended.

These days football 'experts' provide advice in the columns of newspapers and magazines, and offer to sell forecasting and betting systems which are promoted with all kinds of guarantees of success. Nor has the gambling pundit been slow to make the most of modern technology. There is a multitude of software products for the home computer user. *Caveat emptor !* As in all walks of life, the offerings are of variable quality and worth.

You will find that *Football Fortunes* begins by considering the basics of football results prediction before moving on to consider specific theories and strategies in greater depth.

Of course results prediction is by no means an exact science. The outcome of a football match is frequently determined by a single goal, and unforeseen events on the field of play, which reduce the element of skill and increase that of chance, can quickly transform the result of a game. It is for such reasons that the result of *any* game can *never* be a foregone conclusion. Major upsets will always happen. It is of course this uncertainty which helps keep the bookmaker in business. Nevertheless, it is hoped that this book will demonstrate that a logically applied prediction system *can* significantly improve your winning chances. In truth, it may be that 'prediction' is the wrong word. Most methods of 'form analysis' provide a points rating or probability value. Such values should perhaps be seen as a *guide* to your selections... a useful tip ! Ultimately, the wager placed is at the discretion of the gambler.

The mathematical disciplines associated with gambling are those of probability and statistics, and coming to grips with the basics can be both gratifying and financially rewarding.

It was over 400 years ago that the first practical guide to gambling became available. The Italian mathematician Gerolamo Cardano (1501-1576) wrote the *'Book of Games and Chance'* in which the laws of probability governing games of cards and dice were accurately explained.

Incidentally, it seems that Cardano was no mean forecaster. Having predicted the day on which he was to die, he committed suicide and was able to fulfil his prediction precisely !

The mathematical calculations made by Cardano still hold good, and form the fundamentals of our present day understanding of statistical probabilities in gambling.... but our knowledge has grown over the centuries. Blaise Pascal and the Marquis de Laplace were important pioneers in this field. In fact Laplace carried out a scientifically reasoned investigation of the French lottery as long ago as 1812. Today, with advanced analytical techniques and computer technology, increasingly complex statistical theories can be tested and applied.

The laws of chance cannot be ignored, and it makes sense to reduce guess-work as much as possible, so a large part of this book has been devoted to understanding probability and its importance in betting. With such knowledge the punter is better placed to make sound decisions when completing a pools coupon or laying a bet with the bookie. Indeed, to achieve success, the laws of chance must be made to work in *your* favour. The punter must acquire an 'edge', however small.

Football Fortunes considers some approaches to forecasting and betting which might just help establish such an advantage.

The aim is to provide as much information as possible to enable you to mount a serious challenge to the bookmaker. For example, it is useful to know how the bookie prices matches, so you will find within these pages a 'rule of thumb' approach to calculating odds. This is followed by a detailed description of a computer algorithm which prices a fixture list and can be used to simulate the odds found on the bookmakers' coupons.

There is little doubt that the greater the effort made, and knowledge gleaned, the 'luckier' the punter becomes.... but beating the bookie remains a formidable task. To any rational observer it is evident that neither pools companies nor bookmakers are engaged in a philanthropic exercise. Typically, a bookmaker requires the better to put up £11, or more, for every £10 paid out. This income underpins the bookie's business. On top of this the punter must fork out the going rate of betting tax. Furthermore, the rationale behind *fair* betting is that all relevant knowledge is shared between bookmaker and client. In this respect the punter tends to be at a disadvantage, often having access to far less information.

It is also important that all participants in the game itself are seen to be trying their utmost to win. There is little alternative than to assume that this is the case, despite occasional evidence to the contrary.

If all this were not enough, it is little known that, should you be fortunate enough to make the big breakthrough, you can be refused payment... and have no recourse to the law ! As it stands the law does not entertain legal action over gambling debts. This means that the payment of winnings from a successful wager is unenforceable. There is surely a case for the repeal of this centuries-old legislation ?

With such hurdles to overcome, the perpetual optimism of the gambler is astonishing. It seems there is always the expectation that a fundamental flaw or loophole in the system will be discovered and the bookmaker will be taken to the cleaners. Let us hope that this is so.

To some people the sole purpose of gambling is to win money, but it can also be regarded as a pleasurable, intellectual exercise. The gambler is frequently warned to bet only with money which he or she can afford to lose. This may be true. It is certainly the case that if one's financial circumstances are such that winning becomes the be all and end all, there is every chance that good judgement will be impaired and betting will become, not an agreeable pastime, but an obsession. It is surely best to bet for pleasure, while retaining the hope that 'serious money' will be a by-product of your efforts.

It should always be remembered that it is the gambler who decides *when* and *how* to bet. In fact this is *the* power of the punter. It should be exercised wisely. It pays to look for the best bet. If uncertain, then do not bet. Conversely, if an attractive price is offered, and you feel confident, don't be afraid to increase your wager.

In *Football Fortunes* you will find a lengthy article dealing with the basics of placing bets with your local bookmaker and a description of a number of original and innovative wagers. The best of forecasts are worthless unless a sensible betting strategy is applied !

You will notice that the tax rate in several of the practical examples is 10%. Early in 1996 betting tax was reduced to 9%, but the Chancellor of the Exchequer has let it be known that there may be further reductions to come. For this reason, and ease of calculation, it was thought desirable to continue to use the 10% level throughout this book.

As you will gather, there is plenty here for the fixed-odds punter, but the poolites have not been neglected. There is a summary of the history of the pools in Britain and the fundamentals of football pools betting are clearly explained.... again with practical examples of coupon entries.

For those with an interest in computing, there is a description of a modern computerised prediction system, including program code which can be used to list betting 'permutations'. The computer is an ideal forecasting tool, and several of the prediction methods described in the first part of this publication are most efficiently tackled through the use of a computer. This book also contains a comprehensive list of sites on the World Wide Web which will interest both the soccer enthusiast and gambler.

Incidentally, for a first-rate description of the role of the computer in gambling, look no further than that excellent book *'The Punter's Revenge'* by Tony Drapkin and Richard Forsyth.

It is earnestly hoped that *Football Fortunes* will be of value to both the experienced gambler and the newcomer to forecasting, betting and computing. Selection and strategy are the keys to success in a high-risk business. Success cannot of course be guaranteed, but a systematic approach to form analysis, and a judicious choice of bets will, without doubt, significantly improve *your* fortunes.

Forth Dimension
28 Macbeth Road
Dunfermline.
KY11 4EG

This is the first edition of Football Fortunes. There are undoubtedly more to come. Consequently, contributions from readers are most welcome, and if considered suitable will be included in the next publication.
Write and let us know about forecasting systems you have tried out, and how they have fared. Or perhaps you have a favourite bet which has been particularly successful, and would like to share your good fortune !

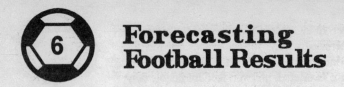

Forecasting Football Results

In football results prediction there can be no certainties and it is futile to seek any. There are however, degrees of likelihood, or probabilties. Indeed the science of probability can be applied to practically any event. Of course some games, such as dice, cards or chess, are more susceptible to probabilistic analysis than others and there are clearly special problems in reducing events involving human behaviour, such as a soccer match, to mathematical formulae. It might be appropriate, on a scale of difficulty, to rate football match prediction at a similar level to weather forecasting.

This meteorological analogy is not so strange as it might first seem, for success in results forecasting is also achieved through the accumulation of historical data and its intelligent and imaginative interpretation.

By gathering and sifting through past records, new forecasting ideas are formulated, while the continuous assessment and refinement of existing strategies will often lead to improved forecasting performance.

Predictive factors and success rate - figure 1

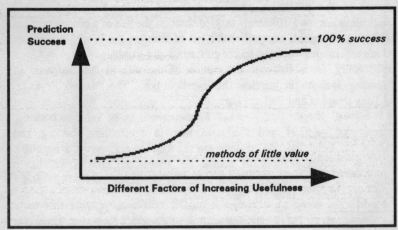

Ideally the football results forecaster would wish to consider the contribution of *all* predictive factors and assess their value. The predictive power of each could be quantified and prediction success expressed as a function of the forecasting method (figure 1).

In reality there are difficulties. Different methods may generate contradictory forecasts, and if several factors are combined some kind of weighting system becomes necessary. Also, as you read through *Football Fortunes*, it will become clear that the vast amount of data, which relates to the strengths and weaknesses of football teams, must be efficiently stored and manipulated. This is most easily achieved through the use of a computer, the ideal forecasting tool.

Ultimately it is up to the individual to consider the merits, or otherwise, of each approach to forecasting. Some methods will be favoured more than others. To help in your efforts, the forecasting process, summarised in figure 2, is considered in detail over the following pages.

The forecasting process - figure 2

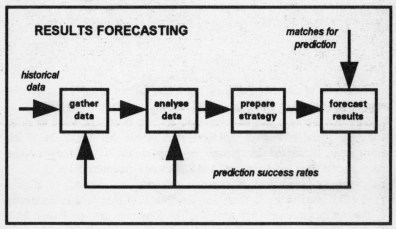

GATHERING DATA

Historical data provides the raw material for the development of a forecasting system or computer algorithm, and as a first step it is useful to identify the *factors* considered likely to influence the outcome of a game of football. In doing so, although it quickly becomes apparent that certain material can be put to little practical use, it will be discovered that there is much information which *can* be accurately measured and analysed with a view to preparing a forecasting system.

There are many sources of information. In addition to newspapers, magazines and football yearbooks, there are associations of statisticians who are able to provide a wealth of material. For the computer user there are databases of match results dating from the last century. Whatever the source, it is such information, plus a basic understanding of the game itself, which will suggest the factors most likely to influence results.

Note, if you are a computer user, the accumulated data will generally be represented in the form of 'variables'.

In a programming sense a variable may be regarded as a symbol which can take on different values within a computer application. For example a variable in a forecasting algorithm might be used to represent league division points.

It will be found that many variables are a measure of individual team strengths and that arithmetic operations are carried out directly on these values to establish the superiority of one team over another.

It must be accepted that there are many potentially useful factors which are not easy to quantify and would prove difficult to consider in any forecasting system. One reason for this is that the forecaster cannot be assured of ready access to the relevant information. Such factors include the influence of adverse weather conditions, injuries to players, suspensions, new signings, tactical changes, internal club 'strife', the state of the pitch, etc. In addition, an assessment of the effects of these particular factors requires a *subjective* judgement on the part of the forecaster, which is difficult to quantify.

Readers may be surprised to learn that, to help overcome some of these problems, there now exist 'football intelligence networks', in which information is shared by groups of like-minded football fans, who communicate their local expertise and knowledge over the telephone !

Fortunately, a good deal of valuable information *is* readily available, without the need to go to these lengths. Much of this data is eminently suitable for measurement and analysis. The forecaster can use league table placings, league points, total goals scored and lost, goal difference, and sequences and proportions of wins, draws and losses, and much more. It could also prove beneficial to consider the results of previous encounters between teams, particularly in the case of cup games or local derbies. In the latter stages of a soccer season an attempt might be made to assess the impact of imminent promotion or relegation on the outcome of matches.

These ideas are far from exhaustive, and many readers will have their own thoughts about what provides good, or indifferent, forecasting material.

Finally, it should be noted that, in any book on the subject of sport results forecasting, you will frequently come across the term 'form'. The form of a football team should be thought of as a representation of a team's previous performances, which it is hoped reflects *current* ability or potential.

In fact form could simply be seen as a mental representation, a subjective feeling about the skill of a team ..... but is of course a much more useful concept if it can be assigned a numerical value. This is not difficult to achieve. As will be shown, many values, such as league points or goals scored, are easily obtained and can be manipulated using pencil and paper, or as variables within a computer program.

DATA ANALYSIS

As we have seen, the first stage in the forecasting process is to identify and accumulate useful information. The next step is to see that the data is analysed and utilised to the best advantage. For example the material might be used to establish trends, compute numerical 'form' ratings, or to calculate ratios of homes, draws and losses for conversion to probabilities and betting odds. In each case it is hoped that, by analysing a *series* of past events, standards can be achieved by which to judge the prospects of the occurrence of *individual*, future events.

If trends are examined they may involve long-term or short-term patterns. As an example of the latter, it might be observed that, in a certain league division, after consecutive home win and away draw, the next home result is a home team victory in 51% of matches played. This knowledge can then be applied within a forecasting system.

In any system using match sequences it can also be useful to distinguish underlying trends from seasonal changes, or other kinds of fluctuations. There may well be considerable differences in statistical patterns at the start and end of a season, or for matches in different league divisions.

Lastly, it must be remembered that the effectiveness of different rating systems is most easily compared in terms of prediction success rates. It is important that comprehensive records are maintained, and a thorough analysis of prediction success and failure carried out on a regular basis.

FORECASTING STRATEGIES

There are many approaches to forecasting. Some strategies are more successful than others, while most will benefit from a continuous fine tuning or refinement to achieve optimum performance. The most basic of systems is that which makes use of the relative position of teams in the football league division tables which regularly appear in our newspapers and on television. It is this method which is the first to be considered.

League Ranking

The football leagues apply a well-established formula to rate soccer teams. They have sufficient confidence in the system to use it to decide which teams are to be relegated or promoted at the end of each season .... although it will quickly becomes clear that, as a forecasting tool, league ranking alone has limited potential. Consider the following 'rule of thumb' approach to results forecasting which might be adopted by an aspiring student of form.

League position heuristic - figure 3

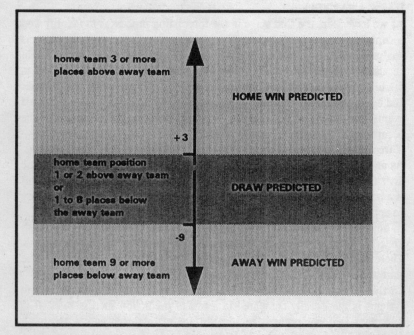

home team 3 or more places above away team

HOME WIN PREDICTED

+3

home team position 1 or 2 above away team or 1 to 8 places below the away team

DRAW PREDICTED

-9

home team 9 or more places below away team

AWAY WIN PREDICTED

In the first instance the predicted winner of a football match might be judged to be any team which is ranked six or more places above its opposition in the table. A positional difference of less than six would indicate a draw prediction. However such a simplistic approach is unlikely to satisfy even the novice forecaster. A superficial analysis of past results will soon reveal that an adjustment of some kind is necessary to reflect *home advantage*. Consequently it might be decided that, for the team playing on its own ground, superiority over the opposition of only three or more league division placings is sufficient to predict a home victory. Conversely, achieving a victory away from home is a greater challenge. An away win could be predicted where the away team is ranked nine places or more above the home team. Intermediate differences would suggest that a draw is on the cards. Such a system can be represented diagramatically (figure 3).

It is evident that over the first month or so of each new season, until a meaningful pecking order has been

Forecasts using league position - figure 4

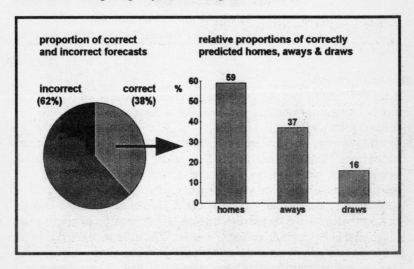

established, this approach is of little worth. In fact an analysis of such a strategy over one month in a recent UK football season suggests that, although a workable system, there is scope for improvement.

Success rates were analysed, and are summarised in figure 4. Of the total predictions made only 38% proved to be correct and, although some tinkering with the formula may give a little more success, any improvement is likely to be minimal.

The problem is that ordinal data of the kind used must always be viewed with caution. Positional numbers are attached only to represent league order and *cannot* show how much better one team is than another. League division rankings do not indicate, for example, that the team in position 10 is twice as bad as that in 5th place, or that the difference between the teams in positions 1 and 2 is in some way comparable to that between 7 and 8. Another drawback is that, at the start of a season, relative league positions change often, but by the end positional changes are less frequent. This means that the *relative contribution* of individual games, and so recent form, diminishes as the season progresses. For the reasons just mentioned, it is not a legitimate statistical practice to carry out arithmetic operations on ordinal data. Consequently league rankings have limited value in computer based forecasting.

Notwithstanding the inherit problems of dealing with ordinal data, there are some valuable lessons to be learned from the league ranking heuristic. In particular the need was demonstrated for an adjustment of some kind which reflects home team advantage. This method also emphasises a recurrent feature of all prediction systems, namely, home wins are easier to predict than away wins, which in turn are better forecast than draws.

League Points

It has been shown that the use of league placings has limited potential in results forecasting. However the *quantitative* measure of league division points is more useful.

Typically, points are allocated as follows. At the start of a new soccer season each team has zero points. Thereafter, for each game played, a winning team receives three points and a team which draws gains one point. The cumulative total for each team determines its league division status. For predictive purposes it would appear to be a simple enough matter to calculate the league division 'points difference' by subtracting the points total of one team from that of another. This difference could then be converted into one of the three categories, home win, draw or away win. However further consideration soon reveals that such an approach has a number of limitations..... not least of which is of course that, at the start of each new football season, every team has zero points !

It is also clear that, in their calculation, league division points make effective use of only one factor, that is whether a game is won, lost or drawn. Other important variables, such as the comparative quality of the opposing teams, or whether results are achieved at home or away, do not figure in the points allocation. Neither can league points be satisfactorily used in the prediction of 'cup' games, which frequently involve teams from different leagues or divisions.

Rateform Points

Although superior to the use of league placings, it has been pointed out that there are a number of drawbacks associated with the use of league division points as a forecasting criterion. Many of these problems can be overcome by employing a simple points rating system of the sort now described.

This has proved to be a popular and successful approach to football results forecasting. The system, which for convenience has been named 'rateform', has its origins in Professor Elo's book *'The Rating of Chessplayers'*, which in turn was adapted for soccer by Tony Drapkin and Richard Forsyth, and described within their first-rate book *'The Punter's Revenge'* (Chapman & Hall).

It is a system ideally suited to the computer, and is one of several methods applied in the *Football Yearbook* forecasting program.

There are potentially many approaches, but these are the fundamental features ....

1. Each team has a 'points total' which represents its current playing form.

2. The average number of points for individual teams remains constant at 1000.

3. For each match played the home and away teams contribute a percentage of their points to a kitty.

4. The percentage contribution of the home team is greater than that of the away team, and so reflects home advantage.

5. The winning team takes the complete points kitty.

6. Teams which draw share the kitty.

The precise computations are represented by the *pseudocode* in figure 5. Typically the home and away teams might contribute, respectively, 7% and 5% (*variables x and y*) to the kitty. The difference in these percentages represents the advantage to the home team of playing on its own ground, so if the away team overcomes this disadvantage it gains extra points.

It is also the case that the larger the size of the contributions to the kitty the more rapidly will individual team ratings change, and so better reflect recent form.

Some specific examples will help demonstrate how the system operates. Consider three football teams starting out with the points totals shown in figure 6. Each of the teams play Oldham and match results are as indicated.

In *match 1* Blackburn are playing at home. Blackburn and Oldham contribute respectively 7% and 5% of their points totals to the kitty. The contribution of Blackburn being more because, not only have they the larger starting points total, they are also the team playing on their home ground. The kitty now contains 110 points.

Blackburn win the match and take all of the kitty. Oldham receive no points. The nett gain to Blackburn is +24 points. This is the value of the kitty *less* the initial contribution. Oldham have sustained a nett loss of -24 points. You will see that the points average of 1000 is undisturbed.

In the first match the overall gain to Blackburn has been quite small. They have won at home against poor opposition.

In *match 2*, Oldham, now the home team, continue to do badly and are once again defeated. In this case both teams began with a low points total, but by winning away from home West Ham have gained extra points.

Pseudocode to update 'rateform' points totals - figure 5

CALCULATING 'RATEFORM' POINTS (1)

The variables are shown in *italics*

The HOME team begins with a points total of *htot*
The AWAY team begins with a points total of *atot*

For each match played the home team contributes *x*% of its points and the away team contributes *y*%   (*x* is greater than *y*).

The actual points contributions of the home and away teams are represented by *hgives* and *agives* respectively.
  hgives = *x*% of *htot*   *agives* = *y*% of *atot*
  kitty = *hgives* + *agives*

The number of points each team receives from the kitty is represented by *hgets* and *agets*.
 If a home win then
   hgets = *kitty*   *agets* = 0
 If an away win then
   hgets = 0   *agets* = *kitty*
 If drawn game then
   hgets = *kitty* / 2 (rounded down)   *agets* = *kitty* - *hgets*
   (if *kitty* is an odd number the away team gets the extra point)

The nett gain or loss to each team is *hnett* and *anett*.
  hnett = *hgets* minus *hgives*   *anett* = *agets* minus *agives*

Finally new points totals are calculated for each team.
  htot = *htot* plus *hnett*   *atot* = *atot* plus *anett*

Finally, *match 3* shows one possible consequence of a draw. Manchester United have drawn at home against Oldham, but have actually *lost* points. It was clearly a game they should have won ! Oldham, on the other hand, have greatly benefited from drawing away from home against top opposition.

So, using this system, the final points allocation is determined by the result, the relative quality of the opposing teams, and whether wins or draws are secured at home or away.

The individual team ratings (at least for teams which remain in the same division) are carried forward from one season to the next. How quickly they change over

Examples of 'rateform' result to points conversion - figure 6

CALCULATING 'RATEFORM' POINTS (2)

Starting points ....

Blackburn 1232	Each to play Oldham (478 points)
Man Utd 1804	
West Ham 486	

Match 1. Blackburn v Oldham - result HOME win

Blackburn (home)
1232 pts X 0.07 = 86
From kitty, a win gives 110
Nett gain +24

Oldham (away)
478 pts X 0.05 = 24
From kitty, a loss gives 0
Nett Loss -24

Kitty
110

Match 2. Oldham v West Ham - result AWAY win

Oldham (home)
478 pts X 0.07 = 33
From kitty, a loss gives 0
Nett Loss -33

West Ham (away)
486 pts X 0.05 = 24
From kitty, a win gives 57
Nett Gain +33

Kitty
57

Match 3. Man Utd v Oldham - result DRAWN game

Man Utd (home)
1804 pts X 0.07 = 126
From kitty, a draw 75
Nett Loss -51

Oldham (away)
478 pts X 0.05 = 24
From kitty, a draw gives 75
Nett Gain +51

Kitty
150

Final points ....

Blackburn 1256	Oldham 472
Man Utd 1753	
West Ham 519	

---

the season depends upon the size of the contributions to the kitty. If these percentage values remain constant, so too does the comparative contribution of each football match result towards overall form. However

16

there may be advantages in varying this value as the season progresses. For instance it could be argued that by having a larger kitty contribution at the *start* of a new season the *current form* of each team can be more quickly established. There is no doubt that the winning potential of football teams varies considerably from one season to another, the form of one year being a poor guide to that of the next. For this reason, as far as relegated and promoted teams are concerned, there seems little use in retaining the previous season's points totals when they move to a new division. It is also clear that, as the years pass, there is insufficient interaction between teams from different divisions to justify this. This leads to the conclusion that it is probably best to allocate an *average* set of points, ie 1000, to newly promoted or relegated teams. Such teams are then placed mid-way in their new division, and by increasing kitty contributions over the first few weeks of the season their true status can quickly become established.

Up to now consideration has been given to the calculation of individual 'rateform' points. The next step is to use these values to predict results.

It will probably come as no surprise that **points difference**, that is home team points *minus* away team points, is the basic forecasting unit used in the 'rateform' system. *(You will have gathered that the use of a points differential, the 'gap' between teams, is a popular approach in many forecasting systems).* Figure 7 shows some 'rateform' predictions.

Examples of 'rateform' predictions - figure 7

'RATEFORM' PREDICTIONS

Points totals ....

Blackburn	1256
Man United	1753
West Ham	519
Oldham	472

Match 1. **Man U v Blackburn**
1753 minus 1256 = Points Difference of +497 .... a HOME is forecast

Match 2. **Oldham v Blackburn**
472 minus 1256 = Points Difference of -784 ..... an AWAY is forecast

Match 3. **West Ham v Oldham**
519 minus 472 = Points Difference of +47 .... a DRAW is forecast

(note : no adjustment has been made for home advantage)

It can be seen that the size of the points difference determines the prediction category into which each match falls. For example it might be decided that any differences of 200 or more should be classified as a potential home win, and of 200 or less an away win. Any intermediate values to be draw predictions.

Extract form *Yearbook* of 'rateform' predictions - figure 8

Predictions with Results
Using rateform points for matches played 08/04/95
The Chi-square Test

Contingency Table (3 X 3)

Predicted Results	Actual Homes	Actual Draws	Actual Aways	Actual Correct%	Expected Correct%
Homes=24	18*	4	2	75.00	48.28
Draws=17	7	4*	6	23.53	22.41
Aways=17	3	5	9*	52.94	29.31
Total 58	28	13	17	53.45	35.14

denotes correct prediction

Improvement over Chance%
Homes=55.34   Draws=4.99   Aways=80.62   Total=52.10

Chi=14.816   Degrees of freedom = 4

Probability distribution for Chi-square...

.05	.02	.01	.001
9.488	11.66	13.27	18.46

Since 14.816 is greater than the critical level of 13.27 there is a significant relationship between predictions and results with probability level p<.010

As it stands this method does not consider home team advantage, which is of course the cause of the larger proportion of home wins compared to aways or draws. The home advantage might be judged to be the equivalent of a bonus of 50 points to the team playing on its own ground. This value can be added to the points difference, or the same effect achieved by adjusting the forecasting parameters to +150 and -250 points. *(In practice yet another adjustment is necessary.... where cup matches are being played in which the opposing teams come from different divisions).*

In figure 8 some 'rateform' predictions have been taken directly from the *Yearbook* software. It is a small sample, only 58 matches, and the success

rate for homes and aways is exceptionally good
*For those with an interest in statistical testing the Chi
value has been given, and indicates a significant
relationship between predictions and results.*

It is always a useful exercise, and has obvious practical

'Rateform' predictions ranked as homes - figure 9

Sorted Home Predictions
with Results and Points Difference
Using rateform points for matches played 08/04/95

Result and points difference(+/-pd)
(ranked from best home rating)

result	+/-pd	result	+/-pd	result	+/-pd
H *	1433	a	324	a	-169
H *	1098	H *	318	d	-204
d	961	H *	271	H *	-238
d	960	H *	230	H *	-244
H *	960	d	177	d	-250
H *	862	a	168	a	-277
H *	703	H *	89	H *	-317
d	642	H *	-8	a	-388
H *	585	d	-33	d	-517
H *	543	a	-42	a	-578
H *	539	H *	-44	a	-724
H *	521	H *	-67	d	-758
H *	468	H *	-72	a	-770
H *	467	H *	-89	d	-915
a	442	a	-92	a	-1046
H *	435	d	-118	a	-1047
d	430	a	-122	a	-1468
H *	374	d	-153	a	-1588
H *	357	a	-162		
H *	340	H *	-167		

* asterisk shows Home result

The Point Biserial
Correlation Coefficient(CCpb)=0.4763
Significance levels for two-tailed test...

.05	.025	.01	.005
0.231	0.273	0.322	0.354

*Since 0.4763 is greater than the critical level 0.354
there is a positive correlation between ratings and
predictions with probability level p<.005*

value, to sort predictions in order of points difference. This has been done in figure 9, which provides a list of the 'best to worst' home forecasts. There is clearly a strong *correlation* between points difference and correct forecasts, and of the top twenty sorted forecasts, *fifteen* were indeed homes.

Points differences and actual match results - figure 10

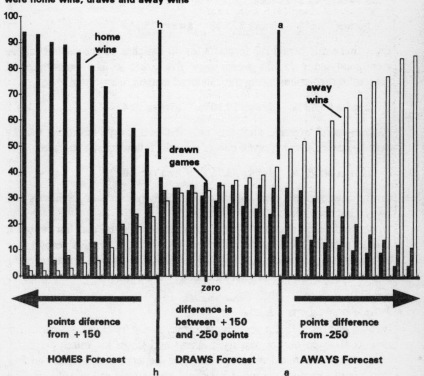

PREDICTION POINTS AND MATCH RESULTS

% of forecasts of which the results were home wins, draws and away wins

It can be seen that, by using the points difference variable, it is an easy matter to identify the top home, draw and away predictions.

In fact the 'rateform' system has been tested over many years and the data analysed.

The histogram in figure 10 shows the changing likelihood of *correct* forecasts as the size of the points difference rises and falls. The diagram also shows the relative proportions of home, draw and away results which occur at the different levels of points difference.

It will be observed that within the 'Draws Forecast' region *(ie between h and a)*, a draw is 'just about' the most probable of the *three* results. However, by far the *majority* of the 'best' draw forecasts will actually turn out as *either* home wins *or* away wins. Draws are without doubt the most difficult of results to predict.

The following statistics may be of interest. Since season 1990-91 the proportion of each type of football result (within the major English and Scottish leagues) has been .....

homes 47.5%   draws 27.0%   aways 25.5%

Over that same period the forecasts for *all* matches on the **pools coupons** were analysed *(11,600 games over five years)*. The proportions of successful predictions, using the 'rateform' method, were found to be ....

homes 57.83%   draws 29.16%   aways 39.45%

A more useful exercise, analysing only the 'best rated' predictions *(ie the best 10 homes, 8 draws and 6 away)* gave the following success rates ....

homes 60.90%   draws 33.76%   aways 51.05%

So the improvement over chance expectations is excellent for homes and aways, but considerably lower for draws.

Undoubtedly the 'rateform' system works, although the real test is that it should provide a consistent return on your wagers. In this respect, the betting strategy is crucial. On page 94, a practical approach to betting using 'rateform' predictions, has been described in some detail.

Win, Draw, Loss - Ratio

It could be argued that a possible deficiency in the 'rateform' system is that the actual *proportion* of past wins, draws and losses for games played by each team is not considered. For example a sequence of four wins and four losses *might* produce a similar 'rateform' points total as eight draws. The solution is to employ a method which considers the *ratio* of past results of each kind and produces a numerical value which represents the *statistical probability* that a team will win, draw or lose.

For instance, it might be found that, of all of the home games played by one team over a specified period, 9 were wins, 2 were draws and 5 losses. Out of the 16 games played the proportions of each result are ....

homes 56.25%   draws 12.50%   aways 31.25%

Similar calculations can be carried out for the opposing away team and the values merged. The final figures can then be thought of as the probability of the future occurrence of each type of result and used to make match predictions. In addition, percentage values such as these can be converted directly into betting odds and, it is hoped, profitably compared with the odds compiled by a bookmaker.

Note : An in-depth analysis of this approach is left until later, when 'Football Fortunes' considers 'Probabilities and Odds' (see page 70).

Sequences

There are many ways to make use of match sequences. The two examples which follow base predictions upon a *short* series of past results, and as such can be said to represent 'recent' form. In addition, form is depicted as a function of the *changing* pattern of results over time, unlike many approaches, such as that just described, which consider the occurrence of wins, draws and losses without regard to the *order* of play.

The first example allocates points for wins and draws as shown below, although the values chosen are at the discretion of the forecaster ....

```
home win = 3      home draw = 1
away win = 4      away draw = 2
```

(Note that the usual notation of H=home, A=away, W=win, D=draw and L=loss, will be applied in this and subsequent examples).

Consider a prediction based upon a five match sequence. The last five *home* results of the team playing at home, are compared with the last five *away* results of the opposition, who are of course playing away from home. The most recent result is to the right in each case, and points are allocated as follows ....

```
home team.. W W D L W      away team.. D D L W L
(home games) 3+3+1+0+3=10   (away games) 2+2+0+4+0=8
```

The home team total *less* the away team total, 10 minus 8 in this instance, *could* provide a 'points difference' which would in turn be used to categorise the forecast as a home, draw or away. The drawback is that the *playing sequence* (chronological order) does not figure in the calculation. Whatever the order of past results, the added home, draw and away points

22

would always give the same total.

To reflect the change in form over time, greater emphasis must be placed upon more recent results. To achieve this use a simple 'weighting' system. *Each win and draw points value is multiplied by its ordinal number in the match sequence.* The points allocated to the fifth match *(ie the last game played)* are multiplied by 5, the fourth by 4, and so on. Continuing our example the allocated points are ....

```
home team.. W W D L W    ( not weighted = 3+3+1+0+3=10 )
 Weighted  =  (3X1)+(3X2)+(1X3)+(0X4)+(3X5)=27

away team.. D D L W L    ( not weighted = 2+2+0+4+0=8 )
 Weighted  =  (2X1)+(2X2)+(0X3)+(4x4)+(0X5)=22
```

The points difference now becomes **27 minus 22** = **5**.

In the *unweighted* calculation the forecast might have been a draw, while the *weighted* forecast, which it is believed better reflects current form, could be a home win. The exact categorisation will naturally depend upon the parameters set by the forecaster. It might be decided that a points difference greater than +3 is to be a home win and less than zero an away win. This means values from 0 to 3 inclusive suggest a draw. This choice of parameters includes the effect of home advantage.

The 'raw data' required for your forecasts is conveniently accessible in newspapers or sporting publications, and the calculations can easily be made with pencil and paper, or hand-held calculator.

The methodology behind the next approach to the use of sequences in forecasting is rather more complex, and in the initial collation and analyses of data a computer proved indispensable.

The concept is not new. Some readers may recall the 'POOLOGS' of the 1950s; although interest in this method was greatly revived by the articles of Professor Frank George, and his book *'Football Pools and How To Win'*. Professor George analysed results over two, three or four games, naming sequences of matches, respectively, dyads, triads and quadrads. The following pages examine the use of the so-called triad in match prediction.

In general, football teams play alternate home and away matches, and it is frequently the case that, in arriving at a prediction, the home record of the home team is compared with the away record of the opposing away team. This was done in the previous example. However there is no evidence to suggest that the analysis of *all* consecutive matches, *whether they be home or away,* should not provide equally valid material upon which to base forecasts. Indeed this may have several advantages. In particular, recent form will be more accurately represented. Assuming games are played on a weekly basis, a three match sequence will have been completed in little more than two weeks, while the use of three homes versus three aways for each prediction requires results from a series of games covering at least four, and possibly five, weeks.

In figures 11 and 12 every possible combination of three consecutive match results (216 different sequences in total) has been listed for all English league divisions from seasons 1985 to 1994. This data, covering ten years, gives us just short of 39,000 triads.

A glance at figure 11 will help explain the idea. This table shows the frequencies of home wins, home draws and home losses occurring after two consecutive matches (a dyad). Take the first line. After a home win and an away loss (the dyad HW,AL), the frequency and proportions of the three possible *home results* which followed this dyad are listed in the adjacent columns. Thus the triad which *began* **HW,AL** was *completed* by home results in the following proportions ....

HW=47.386%   HD=26.188%   HL=26.426%

These are the ratios which provide the basis of our predictions.

It can now be said, for example, that after a home win and an away loss the probability of a home win in the next game is **47.386%**. Of course this observation is of limited worth, as around 47.5% of *all* matches played do, on average, end up as home wins. However, from the forecaster's viewpoint, other triad sequences can provide potentially valuable material.

Although great caution must be exercised, due to the infrequent occurrence of certain sequences, the following triads appear in proportions which depart quite markedly from average, or chance, expectations.

Note that in all cases the most recent result is to the *right,* and it is this, the last result, which determines the category into which the triad falls ....

home win & %	home draw & %	Home loss & %
HW,AW,HW=52.488	AL,HD,HD=30.221	HD,AL,HL=30.097
HW,AD,HW=51.362	HL,AW,HD=28.970	AD,AL,HD=29.038
HD,AD,HW=50.136	AD,HL,HD=28.859	AL,HL,HL=29.422
AW,HW,HW=53.774	HW,HW,HD=29.105	HW,HD,HL=30.909
AD,HW,HW=52.839	HL,HW,HD=30.509	HL,HD,HL=36.111
AW,AW,HW=56.667	HD,HL,HD=29.787	HL,HL,HL=36.000
HW,HL,HW=54.098	HD,HD,HD=31.250	
HD,HW,HW=56.667	HL,HL,HD=36.000	

In figure 11 the third result in the triad is that for a home game. A similar listing in figure 12 shows triads where an *away match* completes the sequence. The next step is to combine the home and away data and create

TRIADS English League
All Divisions 1985 to 1994 inclusive (10 seasons)

HOME RESULTS WHICH COMPLETE TRIADS

home team dyad	Home Wins tot.	%	Home Draws tot.	%	Home Losses tot.	%	Dyads tot.	%	order
(i)	(ii)	(iii)	(iv)	(v)	(vi)	(vii)	(viii)	(ix)	(x)
HW,AL	997	47.386	551	26.188	556	26.426	2104	10.806	1
HW,AW	675	52.488	350	27.216	261	20.296	1286	06.605	2
HL,AL	554	43.281	364	28.438	362	28.281	1280	06.574	3
HW,AD	641	51.362	337	27.003	270	21.635	1248	06.409	4
HD,AL	544	44.013	320	25.890	372	30.097	1236	06.348	5
AL,AL	452	43.337	292	27.996	299	28.667	1043	05.357	6
AL,HW	486	49.846	269	27.590	220	22.564	975	05.007	7
HD,AD	370	50.136	189	25.610	179	24.255	738	03.790	8
HD,AW	326	46.638	198	28.326	175	25.036	699	03.590	9
AW,HW	342	53.774	169	26.572	125	19.654	636	03.266	10
AD,HW	335	52.839	167	26.341	132	20.820	634	03.256	11
HL,AD	290	46.474	170	27.244	164	26.282	624	03.205	12
AD,AL	269	43.883	166	27.080	178	29.038	613	03.148	13
AL,HL	256	42.314	171	28.265	178	29.422	605	03.107	14
AL,AD	255	43.294	178	30.221	156	26.486	589	03.025	15
AL,AD	271	47.130	149	25.913	155	26.957	575	02.953	16
HL,AW	253	44.154	166	28.970	154	26.876	573	02.943	17
AL,AW	241	47.629	130	25.692	135	26.680	506	02.599	18
AW,AL	238	47.791	131	26.305	129	25.904	498	02.558	19
AD,HD	164	47.536	98	28.406	83	24.058	345	01.772	20
AD,AD	157	45.906	88	25.731	97	28.363	342	01.756	21
AD,AW	155	49.839	79	25.402	77	24.759	311	01.597	22
AW,HD	148	47.742	79	25.484	83	26.774	310	01.592	23
AW,AD	150	49.180	75	24.590	80	26.230	305	01.566	24
AW,AW	170	56.667	78	26.000	52	17.333	300	01.541	25
AD,HL	135	45.302	86	28.859	77	25.839	298	01.530	26
AW,HL	134	46.528	74	25.694	80	27.778	288	01.479	27
HW,HW	66	49.254	39	29.105	29	21.642	134	00.688	28
HW,HL	33	54.098	14	22.951	14	22.951	61	00.313	29
HD,HW	34	56.667	13	21.667	13	21.667	60	00.308	30
HL,HW	26	44.068	18	30.509	15	25.424	59	00.303	31
HW,HD	27	49.091	11	20.000	17	30.909	55	00.282	32
HD,HL	22	46.809	14	29.787	11	23.404	47	00.241	33
HL,HD	17	47.222	6	16.667	13	36.111	36	00.185	34
HD,HD	15	46.875	10	31.250	7	21.875	32	00.164	35
HL,HL	8	32.000	9	36.000	8	32.000	25	00.128	36

HW = 9256 47.540% HD = 5258 27.006% HL = 4956 25.455%

Home Prediction Triads = 19470

TRIADS English League
All Divisions 1985 to 1994 inclusive (*10 seasons*)

AWAY RESULTS WHICH COMPLETE TRIADS

away team dyad	Away Wins tot.	%	Away Draws tot.	%	Away Losses tot.	%	Dyads tot.	%	order
(i)	(ii)	(iii)	(iv)	(v)	(vi)	(vii)	(viii)	(ix)	(x)
AL,HW	520	24.774	569	27.108	1010	48.118	2099	10.777	1
AL,HL	292	22.601	308	23.839	692	53.560	1292	06.633	2
AD,HW	382	30.008	305	23.959	586	46.033	1273	06.536	3
AL,HD	326	25.935	349	27.765	582	46.301	1257	06.454	4
AW,HW	344	28.313	355	29.218	516	42.469	1215	06.238	5
HW,HW	317	29.083	302	27.706	471	43.211	1090	05.596	6
HW,AL	243	24.059	283	28.020	484	47.921	1010	05.185	7
AW,HD	195	27.778	203	28.917	304	43.305	702	03.604	8
AD,HD	172	25.749	169	25.299	327	48.952	668	03.430	9
AD,HL	156	23.601	168	25.416	337	50.983	661	03.394	10
HW,AD	152	24.398	176	28.250	295	47.352	623	03.198	11
HD,AL	160	26.144	170	27.778	282	46.078	612	03.142	12
HW,HD	162	26.645	171	28.125	275	45.230	608	03.122	13
HL,AL	130	21.417	151	24.876	326	53.707	607	03.116	14
AW,HL	142	24.825	140	24.476	290	50.699	572	02.937	15
HW,AW	151	26.916	169	30.125	241	42.959	561	02.880	16
HD,HW	147	26.250	155	27.679	258	46.071	560	02.875	17
HL,HW	115	22.417	156	30.409	242	47.174	513	02.634	18
HW,HL	101	21.862	116	25.108	245	53.030	462	02.372	19
HD,AD	91	25.490	99	27.731	167	46.779	357	01.833	20
HL,HL	87	25.816	89	26.410	161	47.775	337	01.730	21
HD,HD	76	22.687	93	27.761	166	49.552	335	01.720	22
HL,HD	61	18.654	91	27.829	175	53.517	327	01.679	23
HD,AW	93	29.808	98	31.410	121	38.782	312	01.602	24
HD,HL	73	24.013	91	29.934	140	46.053	304	01.561	25
HL,AD	73	24.333	76	25.333	151	50.333	300	01.542	26
HL,AW	65	23.636	76	27.636	134	48.727	275	01.412	27
AL,AL	27	21.600	28	22.400	70	56.000	125	00.642	28
AL,AD	14	20.000	20	28.571	36	51.429	70	00.359	29
AL,AW	12	19.048	14	22.222	37	58.730	63	00.323	30
AD,AL	16	26.667	15	25.000	29	48.333	60	00.308	31
AW,AL	14	25.455	15	27.273	26	47.273	55	00.282	32
AW,AD	17	32.076	15	28.302	21	39.623	53	00.272	33
AW,AW	13	30.952	12	28.571	17	40.476	42	00.216	34
AD,AD	11	27.500	8	20.000	21	52.500	40	00.205	35
AD,AW	11	29.730	7	18.919	19	51.351	37	00.190	36

AW = 4961 25.471%   AD = 5262 27.016%   AL = 9254 47.512%

Away Prediction Triads = 19477

Home Win Probabilities *(using combined home and away triads 1985-1994)*

Away Team Dyads . . . .

Home Dyad	HW HW	HW HD	HW HL	HW AW	HW AD	HW AL	HD HW	HD HD	HD HL	HD AW	HD AD	HD AL	HL HW	HL HD	HL HL	HL AW	HL AD	H A
HW,HW	43.9	46.0	52.2	44.2	47.7	48.1	46.7	49.5	47.0	41.9	47.5	46.6	47.6	52.3	48.2	48.9	50.0	52
HW,HD	43.5	45.6	52.6	43.5	47.5	48.0	46.3	49.5	46.5	40.3	47.1	46.3	47.4	52.9	48.0	48.8	50.1	53
HW,HL	43.8	46.0	53.2	44.1	48.0	48.3	46.9	50.3	47.4	41.3	47.8	46.8	47.9	53.6	48.7	49.7	51.0	53
HW,AW	48.2	50.2	52.6	49.6	50.8	50.5	50.5	51.9	51.3	49.8	51.2	50.4	51.0	52.7	51.5	51.8	52.1	52
HW,AD	47.6	49.4	51.8	48.8	50.0	49.8	49.7	51.0	50.3	48.8	50.3	49.6	50.1	51.8	50.6	50.9	51.2	52
HW,AL	46.0	46.9	48.4	46.5	47.4	47.6	47.1	47.7	47.2	46.3	47.3	47.1	47.3	48.2	47.4	47.5	47.8	48
HD,HW	43.9	46.3	53.4	44.3	48.2	48.4	47.1	50.6	47.8	41.7	48.2	47.0	48.2	54.0	49.1	50.1	51.4	54
HD,HD	43.3	45.3	52.6	43.2	47.3	47.9	46.1	49.3	46.1	39.5	46.8	46.1	47.2	52.9	47.7	48.5	50.0	53
HD,HL	43.4	45.3	52.5	43.3	47.3	47.9	46.1	49.2	46.2	39.8	46.8	46.1	47.1	52.7	47.7	48.4	49.9	53
HD,AW	44.6	46.0	49.2	45.0	47.0	47.4	46.4	47.6	46.5	44.2	46.7	46.4	46.9	48.8	47.0	47.2	47.7	49
HD,AD	46.0	47.9	51.3	47.0	48.9	48.9	48.4	50.0	48.9	46.8	49.0	48.3	48.9	51.2	49.4	49.8	50.2	51
HD,AL	43.6	44.4	46.5	43.7	45.1	45.8	44.7	45.2	44.4	43.0	44.6	44.7	44.9	46.0	44.8	44.9	45.2	47
HL,HW	43.3	45.1	52.0	43.1	47.1	47.7	45.9	48.7	45.7	39.6	46.4	45.9	46.9	52.1	47.2	47.9	49.3	52
HL,HD	43.3	45.3	52.6	43.2	47.3	47.9	46.1	49.3	46.2	39.7	46.8	46.1	47.2	52.9	47.7	48.6	50.0	53
HL,HL	43.0	44.7	52.0	42.5	46.8	47.5	45.5	48.3	45.0	38.3	45.8	45.5	46.5	52.0	46.7	47.3	48.9	52
HL,AW	43.5	44.7	48.1	43.6	45.8	46.6	45.1	46.1	44.8	42.3	45.2	45.1	45.6	47.6	45.5	45.6	46.3	49
HL,AD	44.4	45.9	49.3	44.8	46.9	47.4	46.3	47.5	46.3	43.9	46.6	46.3	46.8	48.9	46.9	47.2	47.7	50
HL,AL	43.2	43.9	45.9	43.2	44.6	45.3	44.1	44.6	43.8	42.4	44.0	44.2	44.4	45.4	44.2	44.2	44.6	46
AW,HW	47.1	49.6	53.5	48.7	50.6	50.2	50.2	52.3	51.3	48.8	51.3	50.0	50.8	53.7	51.7	52.3	52.7	53
AW,HD	44.2	46.1	50.9	44.7	47.5	47.9	46.7	48.7	46.9	43.2	47.2	46.6	47.4	50.7	47.8	48.2	49.0	51
AW,HL	43.9	45.6	50.5	44.2	47.1	47.6	46.2	48.2	46.3	42.5	46.7	46.2	46.9	50.2	47.2	47.6	48.5	51
AW,AW	46.1	49.0	54.5	47.7	50.4	49.9	49.8	52.9	51.3	47.5	51.3	49.6	50.7	55.0	52.0	52.9	53.5	54
AW,AD	44.5	46.5	51.5	45.2	48.0	48.2	47.2	49.4	47.6	43.9	47.9	47.1	47.9	51.4	48.4	49.0	49.8	52
AW,AL	44.6	46.4	50.3	45.2	47.5	47.9	46.9	48.5	47.1	44.3	47.4	46.8	47.5	50.1	47.8	48.1	48.7	51
AD,HW	46.8	49.1	52.9	48.2	50.1	49.8	49.7	51.7	50.6	48.2	50.7	49.5	50.3	53.1	51.1	51.6	52.0	53
AD,HD	44.3	46.1	50.7	44.7	47.4	47.8	46.6	48.5	46.8	43.4	47.2	46.6	47.3	50.4	47.7	48.1	48.8	51
AD,HL	43.7	45.3	50.0	43.8	46.7	47.3	45.8	47.6	45.7	42.0	46.1	45.8	46.5	49.6	46.6	46.9	47.8	50
AD,AW	44.7	46.8	51.7	45.4	48.2	48.4	47.4	49.7	48.0	44.3	48.2	47.3	48.2	51.7	48.8	49.3	50.1	52
AD,AD	43.9	45.5	50.0	44.1	46.8	47.4	46.0	47.7	46.0	42.5	46.4	46.0	46.7	49.6	46.8	47.2	48.0	50
AD,AL	43.5	44.6	47.8	43.4	45.6	46.4	44.9	45.9	44.6	42.2	44.9	45.0	45.4	47.2	45.3	45.4	46.0	48
AL,HW	46.3	48.1	50.9	47.3	48.9	48.9	48.5	49.8	48.9	47.2	49.0	48.4	48.9	50.8	49.3	49.6	50.0	51
AL,HD	43.2	44.3	47.6	43.1	45.4	46.2	44.6	45.6	44.2	41.7	44.6	44.7	45.1	46.9	44.9	45.0	45.7	48
AL,HL	42.9	43.8	47.0	42.6	44.9	45.8	44.1	44.9	43.6	41.1	44.0	44.2	44.5	46.2	44.3	44.3	45.0	48
AL,AW	44.6	46.3	50.2	45.2	47.5	47.8	46.8	48.4	47.0	44.3	47.3	46.8	47.4	49.9	47.7	48.0	48.6	50
AL,AD	44.6	46.2	49.8	45.1	47.2	47.6	46.6	48.0	46.8	44.2	47.0	46.6	47.2	49.4	47.4	47.6	48.2	50
AL,AL	43.3	44.0	46.3	43.2	44.8	45.6	44.3	44.8	43.9	42.3	44.2	44.4	44.6	45.8	44.4	44.5	44.9	47

. . . . . . Away Dyads continued . . . .

Home Dyad	AW HW	AW HD	AW HL	AW AW	AW AD	AW AL	AD HW	AD HD	AD HL	AD AW	AD AD	AD AL	AL HW	AL HD	AL HL	AL AW	AL AD	AL AL
W,HW	43.1	44.3	50.4	47.2	46.5	48.7	46.3	49.0	50.7	49.7	50.0	49.0	48.2	46.6	53.2	52.3	50.0	52.5
W,HD	42.8	43.7	50.6	45.4	44.4	48.2	46.2	49.0	50.8	50.0	50.5	48.7	48.1	46.4	53.4	54.2	50.4	53.9
W,HL	43.0	44.2	51.0	48.5	47.4	50.9	46.4	49.4	51.2	53.1	53.5	51.2	48.3	46.7	53.6	56.5	52.7	55.4
W,AW	47.6	49.2	51.9	52.1	52.0	52.3	49.3	51.3	52.0	52.5	52.5	52.3	49.8	49.4	53.0	52.8	52.4	52.8
W,AD	47.0	48.5	51.2	51.0	50.9	51.2	48.7	50.5	51.2	51.4	51.4	51.2	49.3	48.8	52.5	51.7	51.4	51.8
W,AL	45.6	46.4	48.1	47.3	47.2	47.4	46.9	47.8	48.2	47.5	47.5	47.4	47.8	47.0	49.7	47.7	47.5	47.9
D,HW	43.1	44.4	51.3	50.0	48.7	52.2	46.5	49.6	51.5	54.6	55.0	52.5	48.4	46.8	53.7	57.7	53.8	56.2
D,HD	42.6	43.5	50.5	43.2	42.4	47.1	46.1	48.9	50.8	49.3	50.0	47.8	48.1	46.3	53.4	54.7	50.0	54.1
D,HL	42.6	43.5	50.4	43.8	43.0	47.1	46.1	48.8	50.7	48.8	49.4	47.7	48.1	46.3	53.3	53.6	49.6	53.5
D,AW	44.0	45.0	48.5	46.3	46.1	46.7	46.2	47.8	48.8	46.9	47.0	46.8	47.7	46.4	51.1	47.6	47.1	48.1
D,AD	45.4	46.8	50.4	49.6	49.4	49.9	47.5	49.6	50.5	50.2	50.3	50.0	48.6	47.5	52.3	50.8	50.2	51.0
D,AL	43.2	43.8	46.1	43.9	43.8	44.2	45.0	45.7	46.4	44.2	44.3	44.2	46.6	45.2	48.9	44.7	44.4	45.1
L,HW	42.5	43.4	50.1	42.6	42.0	45.6	45.9	48.6	50.4	46.9	47.5	46.2	48.0	46.2	53.1	51.6	48.1	52.2
L,HD	42.6	43.5	50.5	43.6	42.7	47.3	46.1	48.9	50.8	49.3	50.0	47.9	48.1	46.3	53.4	54.5	50.0	54.0
L,HL	42.3	42.9	49.9	37.3	37.2	42.5	45.8	48.3	50.3	43.5	44.6	43.5	47.9	46.0	53.2	51.1	46.3	52.0
L,AW	43.0	43.7	47.4	43.9	43.8	44.4	44.5	46.7	47.8	44.6	44.7	44.5	47.3	45.6	50.7	45.6	44.9	46.3
L,AD	43.8	44.8	48.5	46.1	45.9	46.5	46.2	47.8	48.8	46.7	46.8	46.6	47.7	46.4	51.3	47.6	47.0	48.1
L,AL	42.9	43.3	45.6	43.2	43.1	43.4	44.7	45.2	45.9	43.5	43.6	43.5	46.3	44.8	48.4	44.0	43.7	44.4
W,HW	46.4	48.3	52.3	52.9	52.7	53.3	48.6	51.3	52.4	53.6	53.7	53.3	49.4	48.8	53.6	54.2	53.5	54.1
W,HD	43.5	44.7	49.7	46.9	46.6	47.7	46.4	48.6	49.9	48.1	48.3	47.8	48.1	46.6	52.4	49.6	48.4	50.1
W,HL	43.2	44.2	49.3	45.8	45.5	46.6	46.1	48.2	49.6	47.1	47.3	46.8	47.9	46.3	52.3	48.7	47.5	49.4
W,AW	45.3	47.3	52.8	54.7	54.1	55.2	48.1	51.3	52.8	56.1	56.2	55.3	49.2	48.3	54.1	57.0	55.7	56.5
W,AD	43.8	45.1	50.2	48.1	47.8	48.9	46.6	49.0	50.4	49.4	49.6	49.0	48.3	46.9	52.7	50.8	49.6	51.2
W,AL	44.0	45.2	49.3	47.2	47.0	47.7	46.5	48.5	49.6	48.0	48.1	47.8	48.1	46.7	52.0	49.0	48.2	49.4
D,HW	46.0	47.8	51.8	52.1	51.8	52.4	48.3	50.8	51.9	52.8	52.8	52.4	49.2	48.5	53.3	53.4	52.7	53.4
D,HD	43.6	44.7	49.5	46.8	46.5	47.5	46.4	48.5	49.8	47.9	48.1	47.7	48.0	46.6	52.3	49.3	48.2	49.8
D,HL	43.0	43.9	48.9	44.7	44.4	45.6	45.9	47.8	49.2	46.0	46.2	45.8	47.8	46.1	52.0	47.6	46.5	48.5
D,AW	44.0	45.3	50.4	48.7	48.4	49.5	46.8	49.2	50.6	50.0	50.1	49.6	48.3	47.0	52.8	51.3	50.1	51.6
D,AD	43.2	44.2	48.9	45.3	45.1	46.1	46.0	47.9	49.3	46.4	46.6	46.3	47.8	46.2	52.0	47.9	46.8	48.6
D,AL	42.9	43.6	47.2	43.7	43.5	44.2	45.3	46.5	47.6	44.3	44.4	44.3	47.2	45.5	50.4	45.3	44.7	45.9
L,HW	45.8	47.1	50.2	49.5	49.3	49.7	47.7	49.5	50.3	49.9	50.0	49.8	48.7	48.2	52.0	50.4	50.0	50.5
L,HD	42.7	43.3	46.9	43.1	43.0	43.6	45.2	46.3	47.4	43.8	43.9	43.8	47.1	45.3	50.3	44.8	44.2	45.5
L,HL	42.4	42.8	46.4	42.2	42.1	42.7	44.8	45.8	46.8	42.8	42.9	42.9	46.8	45.0	50.0	43.9	43.3	44.7
L,AW	44.0	45.1	49.3	47.1	46.9	47.6	46.5	48.4	49.5	47.9	48.0	47.7	48.0	46.7	51.9	48.9	48.1	49.3
L,AD	44.0	45.0	48.9	46.7	46.5	47.1	46.4	48.1	49.2	47.4	47.5	47.2	47.9	46.6	51.6	48.3	47.6	48.7
L,AL	42.9	43.3	45.9	43.2	43.2	43.5	44.8	45.5	46.3	43.6	43.7	43.6	46.5	45.0	49.0	44.2	43.8	44.7

Away Win Probabilities (using combined home and away triads 1985-1994)

Away Team Dyads . . . .

Home Dyad	HW HW	HW HD	HW HL	HW AW	HW AD	HW AL	HD HW	HD HD	HD HL	HD AW	HD AD	HD AL	HL HW	HL HD	HL HL	HL AW	HL AD
HW,HW	28.3	25.7	21.8	25.9	23.9	23.8	25.4	22.4	23.3	27.4	24.4	25.3	22.3	19.5	24.6	23.0	23.5
HW,HD	29.2	27.0	22.8	27.3	24.9	24.4	26.7	23.8	25.1	30.0	26.2	26.5	23.2	20.4	26.5	24.8	25.4
HW,HL	28.8	26.3	22.0	26.5	24.3	24.0	25.9	22.7	23.8	28.7	25.1	25.9	22.5	19.3	25.4	23.5	24.1
HW,AW	24.3	22.3	20.7	22.3	21.6	22.0	22.1	20.8	21.0	22.2	21.4	22.2	20.9	20.0	21.4	20.9	21.1
HW,AD	25.1	23.3	21.7	23.3	22.6	22.7	23.1	21.9	22.1	23.3	22.5	23.1	21.9	21.0	22.5	22.0	22.2
HW,AL	27.3	26.5	25.6	26.5	26.0	25.7	26.4	25.9	26.1	26.9	26.3	26.4	25.6	25.4	26.3	26.1	26.2
HD,HW	28.7	26.2	21.8	26.4	24.2	23.9	25.8	22.5	23.6	28.5	24.9	25.7	22.3	19.1	25.2	23.3	23.9
HD,HD	28.9	26.4	21.9	26.6	24.3	24.0	26.0	22.6	23.8	29.1	25.2	25.9	22.4	18.9	25.5	23.5	24.1
HD,HL	28.8	26.4	22.0	26.6	24.3	24.0	26.0	22.8	23.9	29.0	25.2	25.9	22.5	19.3	25.5	23.6	24.2
HD,AW	27.5	25.8	23.8	25.9	24.7	24.5	25.6	24.3	24.7	26.5	25.2	25.6	23.9	23.0	25.3	24.6	24.8
HD,AD	27.1	25.3	23.3	25.4	24.3	24.1	25.1	23.8	24.2	25.9	24.7	25.1	23.5	22.5	24.7	24.1	24.3
HD,AL	29.6	29.0	27.9	29.1	28.2	27.4	28.9	28.5	28.9	30.0	29.1	28.8	27.8	27.7	29.2	28.9	29.0
HL,HW	28.9	26.5	22.3	26.8	24.5	24.1	26.2	23.1	24.2	29.1	25.5	26.1	22.7	19.7	25.8	24.0	24.5
HL,HD	29.3	27.2	22.9	27.5	25.0	24.5	26.8	24.0	25.3	30.5	26.5	26.7	23.3	20.4	26.8	25.1	25.6
HL,HL	29.1	26.9	22.4	27.1	24.7	24.3	26.5	23.3	24.6	30.0	25.9	26.4	22.9	19.6	26.2	24.3	24.9
HL,AW	28.3	26.8	24.6	26.9	25.6	25.1	26.6	25.3	25.9	27.9	26.3	26.5	24.8	23.9	26.5	25.8	26.0
HL,AD	28.1	26.5	24.4	26.6	25.3	24.9	26.3	25.0	25.5	27.5	26.0	26.2	24.5	23.7	26.1	25.5	25.6
HL,AL	28.6	27.8	26.6	27.9	27.0	26.4	27.7	27.1	27.5	28.6	27.7	27.6	26.6	26.3	27.8	27.5	27.5
AW,HW	25.6	23.1	20.6	23.1	22.0	22.4	22.7	20.7	21.1	23.0	21.8	22.8	20.9	19.3	21.8	20.9	21.2
AW,HD	26.6	26.7	23.8	26.9	25.2	24.7	26.4	24.7	25.4	28.3	26.1	26.4	24.1	22.6	26.3	25.3	25.6
AW,HL	28.8	27.0	24.1	27.2	25.5	24.9	26.8	25.0	25.8	28.8	26.5	26.7	24.3	22.9	26.7	25.8	26.0
AW,AW	26.5	23.6	20.1	23.6	22.1	22.5	23.1	20.2	20.7	23.7	21.8	23.2	20.5	18.0	21.8	20.3	20.8
AW,AD	28.5	26.5	23.6	26.7	25.0	24.6	26.2	24.4	25.1	28.0	25.8	26.2	23.8	22.3	26.0	25.0	25.3
AW,AL	28.1	26.3	24.0	26.4	25.1	24.7	26.1	24.6	25.2	27.4	25.7	26.0	24.1	23.0	25.9	25.1	25.3
AD,HW	26.0	23.7	21.3	23.7	22.6	22.8	23.4	21.5	21.9	23.8	22.5	23.4	21.5	20.1	22.6	21.7	21.9
AD,HD	27.9	25.7	22.8	25.8	24.3	24.1	25.4	23.4	24.0	26.8	24.8	25.4	23.1	21.4	24.9	23.9	24.2
AD,HL	28.4	26.4	23.4	26.5	24.9	24.5	26.1	24.2	24.9	27.9	25.6	26.0	23.7	22.1	25.8	24.8	25.1
AD,AW	28.1	26.0	23.0	26.1	24.5	24.2	25.7	23.7	24.4	27.3	25.1	25.7	23.3	21.6	25.3	24.2	24.5
AD,AD	28.9	27.3	24.6	27.5	25.8	25.1	27.1	25.6	26.3	29.1	26.9	26.9	24.8	23.6	27.1	26.3	26.5
AD,AL	29.1	27.8	26.0	28.0	26.7	25.9	27.7	26.8	27.4	29.3	27.7	27.6	26.0	25.4	27.9	27.4	27.5
AL,HW	26.0	24.1	22.3	24.2	23.3	23.3	23.9	22.6	22.9	24.3	23.3	23.9	22.5	21.6	23.4	22.8	23.0
AL,HD	28.2	26.6	24.5	26.7	25.4	25.0	26.4	25.1	25.6	27.6	26.1	26.3	24.6	23.7	26.2	25.6	25.8
AL,HL	29.2	28.0	26.1	28.2	26.9	26.1	27.9	27.0	27.6	29.6	28.0	27.8	26.2	25.6	28.1	27.6	27.5
AL,AW	28.3	26.7	24.4	26.8	25.4	24.9	26.5	25.1	25.7	27.9	26.2	26.4	24.5	23.5	26.3	25.6	25.8
AL,AD	28.3	26.8	24.7	26.9	25.6	25.1	26.0	25.4	25.9	28.0	26.4	26.5	24.8	23.9	26.5	25.9	26.1
AL,AL	28.9	27.9	26.6	28.1	27.1	26.4	27.8	27.2	27.6	28.9	27.9	27.7	26.6	26.3	28.0	27.6	27.7

.... Away Dyads continued ....

Home Dyad	AW HW	AW HD	AW HL	AW AW	AW AD	AW AL	AD HW	AD HD	AD HL	AD AW	AD AD	AD AL	AL HW	AL HD	AL HL	AL AW	AL AD	AL AL
HW,HW	27.7	26.8	24.2	23.9	24.6	22.8	29.2	25.1	23.3	23.4	23.0	23.2	24.6	25.5	22.5	20.8	21.1	21.6
HW,HD	28.4	28.0	25.4	30.9	31.5	28.2	30.0	26.1	24.2	30.4	29.5	28.7	24.9	26.1	22.9	24.6	24.8	24.4
HW,HL	28.1	27.4	24.6	26.2	27.2	24.1	29.7	25.5	23.5	25.5	24.8	24.8	24.7	25.8	22.6	21.0	21.4	22.0
HW,AW	24.2	22.9	21.7	20.6	20.8	20.5	25.1	22.2	21.4	20.6	20.5	20.6	23.1	23.1	21.5	20.2	20.3	20.4
HW,AD	24.9	23.8	22.6	21.9	22.1	21.8	25.9	23.1	22.3	21.9	21.8	21.9	23.6	23.8	22.1	21.5	21.5	21.6
HW,AL	27.1	26.8	26.1	26.5	26.6	26.4	27.8	26.3	25.8	26.5	26.4	26.4	25.6	26.2	25.0	26.2	26.2	26.2
HD,HW	28.0	27.3	24.5	25.5	26.5	23.5	29.6	25.4	23.4	24.7	24.0	24.2	24.7	25.7	22.6	20.3	20.8	21.6
HD,HD	28.1	27.5	24.7	27.0	28.2	24.1	29.8	25.6	23.5	26.1	25.0	25.0	24.7	25.8	22.6	20.0	20.6	21.7
HD,HL	28.1	27.5	24.7	27.0	28.0	24.5	29.8	25.6	23.6	26.2	25.3	25.2	24.7	25.8	22.6	20.9	21.4	22.1
HD,AW	27.1	26.4	24.9	25.4	25.5	25.1	28.2	25.4	24.3	25.3	25.2	25.2	24.8	25.6	23.5	24.5	24.6	24.5
HD,AD	26.8	26.0	24.5	24.6	24.8	24.3	27.9	25.0	23.9	24.5	24.4	24.4	24.6	25.3	23.2	23.8	23.9	23.9
HD,AL	29.2	29.3	28.4	30.1	30.2	29.9	30.1	28.6	27.8	30.1	30.0	29.9	26.7	28.0	26.3	29.6	29.6	29.3
HL,HW	28.2	27.6	24.9	27.7	28.6	25.4	29.8	25.7	23.8	27.1	26.3	26.1	24.8	25.9	22.7	22.1	22.5	22.8
HL,HD	28.5	28.2	25.5	33.3	33.7	29.7	30.2	26.3	24.2	32.9	31.6	30.2	25.0	26.2	23.0	25.3	25.5	24.8
HL,HL	28.4	27.9	25.1	31.3	32.1	27.5	30.0	26.0	23.9	30.6	29.2	28.2	24.9	26.1	22.8	22.7	23.2	23.3
HL,AW	27.9	27.4	25.9	27.2	27.3	26.8	29.0	26.3	25.1	27.0	26.9	26.9	25.2	26.2	23.9	26.1	26.1	25.9
HL,AD	27.6	27.1	25.6	26.6	26.7	26.2	28.8	26.0	24.9	26.5	26.4	26.3	25.1	26.0	23.8	25.6	25.6	25.5
HL,AL	28.3	28.1	27.2	28.4	28.4	28.2	29.1	27.4	26.7	28.3	28.3	28.2	26.1	27.1	25.4	27.8	27.9	27.7
AW,HW	25.3	23.9	22.1	20.4	20.6	20.1	26.6	22.8	21.7	20.2	20.1	20.3	23.6	23.8	21.6	19.6	19.7	20.0
AW,HD	28.0	27.5	25.5	27.3	27.5	26.6	29.4	26.1	24.6	27.1	26.9	26.8	25.0	26.1	23.4	25.5	25.5	25.3
AW,HL	28.2	27.8	25.8	28.2	28.4	27.4	29.6	26.4	24.9	28.0	27.7	27.6	25.1	26.3	23.5	26.2	26.3	25.9
AW,AW	26.1	24.7	22.2	19.0	19.5	18.6	27.6	23.1	21.6	18.7	18.5	18.9	23.8	24.3	21.6	17.6	17.8	18.6
AW,AD	27.9	27.3	25.3	26.8	27.1	26.1	29.3	25.9	24.4	26.6	26.4	26.3	25.0	26.0	23.3	25.0	25.1	24.9
AW,AL	27.6	27.0	25.3	26.3	26.5	25.9	28.9	25.8	24.6	26.2	26.0	26.0	25.0	25.9	23.5	25.1	25.2	25.0
AD,HW	25.7	24.5	22.7	21.4	21.7	21.2	27.0	23.3	22.2	21.3	21.2	21.3	23.9	24.2	22.0	20.7	20.7	20.9
AD,HD	27.4	26.6	24.5	24.8	25.1	24.3	28.7	25.2	23.8	24.6	24.4	24.4	24.7	25.5	22.9	23.3	23.4	23.4
AD,HL	27.8	27.2	25.2	26.5	26.8	25.8	29.2	25.8	24.3	26.0	26.0	24.9	25.9	23.2	24.7	24.7	24.6	
AD,AW	27.6	26.9	24.8	25.5	25.8	24.9	29.0	25.4	24.0	25.3	25.1	25.1	24.8	25.7	23.0	23.8	23.9	23.9
AD,AD	28.3	28.0	26.1	28.6	28.9	28.0	29.7	26.6	25.2	28.5	28.3	28.1	25.3	26.5	23.8	26.9	26.9	26.6
AD,AL	28.6	28.4	27.0	29.2	29.3	28.7	29.7	27.3	26.2	29.1	28.9	28.8	25.7	27.0	24.7	28.1	28.1	27.8
AL,HW	25.8	24.7	23.4	22.9	23.1	22.7	26.8	23.9	23.0	22.8	22.8	22.8	24.1	24.5	22.6	22.4	22.4	22.5
AL,HD	27.7	27.2	25.7	26.8	26.9	26.4	28.9	26.1	25.0	26.7	26.6	26.5	25.1	26.1	23.8	25.8	25.8	25.6
AL,HL	28.7	28.5	27.2	29.5	29.6	29.1	29.8	27.5	26.4	29.4	29.3	29.2	25.8	27.1	24.8	28.4	28.4	28.1
AL,AW	27.8	27.3	25.7	27.0	27.2	26.6	29.1	26.1	24.9	26.9	26.7	26.7	25.1	26.1	23.7	25.8	25.9	25.7
AL,AD	27.9	27.4	25.9	27.2	27.4	26.8	29.1	26.3	25.2	27.1	27.0	26.9	25.2	26.3	23.9	26.2	26.2	26.0
AL,AL	28.5	28.3	27.3	28.8	28.8	28.5	29.4	27.5	26.7	28.7	28.6	28.6	26.1	27.2	25.3	28.1	28.1	27.9

Draw Probabilities *(using combined home and away triads 1985-1994)*

Away Team Dyads ·

Home Dyad	HW HW	HW HD	HW HL	HW AW	HW AD	HW AL	HD HW	HD HD	HD HL	HD AW	HD AD	HD AL	HL HW	HL HD	HL HL	HL AW	HL AD	HL AL
HW,HW	27.8	28.3	26.0	29.9	28.4	28.1	27.9	28.1	29.7	30.7	28.1	28.1	30.1	28.2	27.2	28.1	26.5	25.6
HW,HD	27.3	27.4	24.6	29.2	27.6	27.6	27.0	26.7	28.4	29.7	26.7	27.2	29.4	26.7	25.5	26.4	24.5	24.5
HW,HL	27.4	27.7	24.8	29.4	27.7	27.7	27.2	27.0	28.8	30.0	27.1	27.3	29.6	27.1	25.9	26.8	24.9	24.7
HW,AW	27.5	27.5	26.7	28.1	27.6	27.5	27.4	27.3	27.7	28.0	27.4	27.4	28.1	27.3	27.1	27.3	26.8	26.4
HW,AD	27.3	27.3	26.5	27.9	27.4	27.5	27.2	27.1	27.6	27.9	27.2	27.3	28.0	27.2	26.9	27.1	26.6	26.3
HW,AL	26.7	26.6	26.0	27.0	26.6	26.7	26.5	26.4	26.7	26.8	26.4	26.5	27.1	26.4	26.3	26.4	26.0	25.9
HD,HW	27.4	27.5	24.8	29.3	27.6	27.7	27.1	26.9	28.6	29.8	26.9	27.3	29.5	26.9	25.7	26.6	24.7	24.6
HD,HD	27.8	28.3	25.5	30.2	28.4	28.1	27.9	28.1	30.1	31.4	28.0	28.0	30.4	28.2	26.8	28.0	25.9	25.2
HD,HL	27.8	28.3	25.5	30.1	28.4	28.1	27.9	28.0	29.9	31.2	28.0	28.0	30.4	28.0	26.8	28.0	25.9	25.2
HD,AW	27.9	28.2	27.0	29.1	28.3	28.1	28.0	28.1	28.8	29.3	28.1	28.0	29.2	28.2	27.7	28.2	27.5	26.7
HD,AD	26.9	26.8	25.4	27.6	26.8	27.0	26.5	26.2	26.9	27.3	26.3	26.6	27.6	26.3	25.9	26.1	25.5	25.3
HD,AL	26.8	26.6	25.6	27.2	26.7	26.8	26.4	26.3	26.7	27.0	26.3	26.5	27.3	26.3	26.0	26.2	25.8	25.6
HL,HW	27.8	28.4	25.7	30.1	28.4	28.2	27.9	28.2	30.1	31.3	28.1	28.0	30.4	28.2	27.0	28.1	26.2	25.3
HL,HD	27.4	27.5	24.5	29.3	27.7	27.6	27.1	26.7	28.5	29.8	26.7	27.2	29.5	26.7	25.5	26.3	24.4	24.5
HL,HL	27.9	28.4	25.6	30.4	28.5	28.2	28.0	28.4	30.4	31.7	28.3	28.1	30.6	28.4	27.1	28.4	26.2	25.4
HL,AW	28.2	28.5	27.3	29.5	28.6	28.3	28.3	28.6	29.3	29.8	28.5	28.4	29.6	28.5	28.0	28.6	27.7	26.8
HL,AD	27.5	27.6	26.3	28.6	27.8	27.7	27.4	27.5	28.2	28.6	27.4	27.5	28.7	27.4	27.0	27.3	26.7	26.1
HL,AL	28.2	28.3	27.5	28.9	28.4	28.3	28.2	28.3	28.7	29.0	28.3	28.2	29.0	28.3	28.0	28.3	27.9	27.3
AW,HW	27.3	27.3	25.9	28.2	27.4	27.4	27.1	27.0	27.6	28.2	26.9	27.2	28.3	27.0	26.5	26.8	26.1	25.8
AW,HD	27.2	27.2	25.3	28.4	27.3	27.4	26.9	26.6	27.7	28.5	26.7	27.0	28.5	26.7	25.9	26.5	25.4	25.1
AW,HL	27.3	27.4	25.4	28.6	27.4	27.5	27.0	26.8	27.9	28.7	26.8	27.1	28.8	26.9	26.1	26.6	25.5	25.1
AW,AW	27.4	27.4	25.4	28.7	27.5	27.6	27.1	26.9	28.0	28.8	26.9	27.2	28.8	27.0	26.2	26.8	25.7	25.2
AW,AD	27.0	27.0	24.9	28.1	27.0	27.2	26.6	26.2	27.3	28.1	26.3	26.7	28.3	26.3	25.6	26.0	24.9	24.8
AW,AL	27.3	27.3	25.7	28.4	27.4	27.4	27.0	26.9	27.7	28.3	26.9	27.2	28.4	26.9	26.3	26.8	26.0	25.6
AD,HW	27.2	27.2	25.8	28.1	27.3	27.4	26.9	26.8	27.5	28.0	26.8	27.1	28.2	26.8	26.3	26.7	26.1	25.6
AD,HD	27.8	28.2	26.5	29.5	28.3	28.1	28.0	28.1	29.2	29.8	28.0	28.0	29.6	28.2	27.4	28.0	27.0	26.1
AD,HL	27.9	28.3	26.6	29.7	28.4	28.2	28.1	28.2	29.4	30.1	28.3	28.2	29.8	28.3	27.6	28.3	27.1	26.2
AD,AW	27.2	27.2	25.3	28.5	27.3	27.4	26.9	26.6	27.6	28.4	26.7	27.0	28.5	26.7	25.9	26.5	25.4	25.1
AD,AD	27.2	27.2	25.4	28.4	27.4	27.5	26.9	26.7	27.7	28.4	26.7	27.1	28.5	26.8	26.1	26.5	25.5	25.2
AD,AL	27.4	27.6	26.2	28.6	27.7	27.7	27.4	27.3	28.0	28.5	27.4	27.4	28.6	27.4	26.8	27.2	26.5	26.0
AL,HW	27.7	27.8	26.8	28.5	27.8	27.8	27.6	27.6	28.2	28.5	27.7	27.7	28.6	27.6	27.3	27.6	27.0	26.6
AL,HD	28.6	29.1	27.9	30.2	29.2	28.8	29.0	29.3	30.2	30.7	29.3	29.0	30.3	29.4	28.9	29.4	28.5	27.5
AL,HL	27.9	28.2	26.9	29.2	28.2	28.1	28.0	28.1	28.8	29.3	28.0	28.0	29.3	28.2	27.6	28.1	27.3	26.6
AL,AW	27.1	27.0	25.4	28.0	27.1	27.3	26.7	26.5	27.3	27.8	26.5	26.8	28.1	26.6	26.0	26.4	25.6	25.3
AL,AD	27.1	27.0	25.5	28.0	27.2	27.3	26.8	26.6	27.3	27.8	26.6	26.9	28.0	26.7	26.1	26.5	25.7	25.4
AL,AL	27.8	28.1	27.1	28.7	28.1	28.0	27.9	28.0	28.5	28.8	27.9	27.9	28.8	27.9	27.6	27.9	27.4	26.8

.... Away Dyads continued ....

Home Diad	AW BW	AW BD	AW HL	AW AW	AW AD	AW AL	AD BW	AD BD	AD HL	AD AW	AD AD	AD AL	AL BW	AL BD	AL HL	AL AW	AL AD	AL AL
BW,BW	29.2	28.9	25.4	28.9	28.9	28.5	24.5	25.9	26.0	26.9	27.0	27.8	27.2	27.9	24.3	26.9	28.9	25.9
BW,BD	28.8	28.3	24.0	23.7	24.1	23.6	23.8	24.9	25.0	19.6	20.0	22.6	27.0	27.5	23.7	21.2	24.8	21.7
BW,HL	28.9	28.4	24.4	25.3	25.4	25.0	23.9	25.1	25.3	21.4	21.7	24.0	27.0	27.5	23.8	22.5	25.9	22.6
BW,AW	28.2	27.9	26.4	27.3	27.2	27.2	25.6	26.5	26.6	26.9	27.0	27.1	27.1	27.5	25.5	27.0	27.3	26.8
BW,AD	28.1	27.7	26.2	27.1	27.0	27.0	25.4	26.4	26.5	26.7	26.8	26.9	27.1	27.4	25.4	26.8	27.1	26.6
BW,AL	27.3	26.8	25.8	26.2	26.2	26.2	25.3	25.9	26.0	26.0	26.1	26.2	26.6	26.8	25.3	26.1	26.3	25.9
BD,BW	28.9	28.3	24.2	24.5	24.8	24.3	23.9	25.0	25.1	20.7	21.0	23.3	26.9	27.5	23.7	22.0	25.4	22.2
BD,BD	29.3	29.0	24.8	29.8	29.4	28.8	24.1	25.5	25.7	24.6	25.0	27.2	27.2	27.9	24.0	25.3	29.4	24.2
BD,HL	29.3	29.0	24.9	29.2	29.0	28.4	24.1	25.6	25.7	25.0	25.3	27.1	27.2	27.9	24.1	25.5	29.0	24.4
BD,AW	28.9	28.6	26.6	28.3	28.4	28.2	25.6	26.8	26.9	27.8	27.8	28.0	27.5	28.0	25.4	27.9	28.3	27.4
BD,AD	27.8	27.2	25.1	25.8	25.8	25.8	24.6	25.4	25.6	25.3	25.3	25.6	26.8	27.0	24.5	25.4	25.9	25.1
BD,AL	27.6	26.9	25.5	26.0	26.0	25.9	24.9	25.7	25.8	25.7	25.7	25.9	26.7	26.8	24.8	25.7	26.0	25.6
HL,BW	29.3	29.0	25.0	29.7	29.4	29.0	24.3	25.7	25.8	26.0	26.2	27.7	27.2	27.9	24.2	26.3	29.4	25.0
HL,BD	28.9	28.3	24.0	23.1	23.6	23.0	23.7	24.8	25.0	17.8	18.4	21.9	26.9	27.5	23.6	20.2	24.5	21.2
HL,HL	29.3	29.2	25.0	31.4	30.7	30.0	24.2	25.7	25.8	25.9	26.2	28.3	27.2	27.9	24.0	26.2	30.5	24.7
HL,AW	29.1	28.9	26.7	28.9	28.9	28.8	25.6	27.0	27.1	28.4	28.4	28.6	27.5	28.2	25.4	28.3	29.0	27.8
HL,AD	28.6	28.1	25.9	27.3	27.4	27.3	25.0	26.2	26.3	26.8	26.8	27.1	27.2	27.6	24.9	26.8	27.4	26.4
HL,AL	28.8	28.4	26.2	28.4	28.5	28.4	26.2	27.4	27.4	28.2	28.1	28.3	27.6	28.1	26.2	28.2	28.4	27.9
AW,BW	28.3	27.8	25.6	26.7	26.7	26.6	24.8	25.9	25.9	26.2	26.2	26.4	27.0	27.4	24.8	26.2	26.8	25.9
AW,BD	28.5	27.8	24.8	25.8	25.9	25.7	24.2	25.3	25.5	24.8	24.8	25.4	26.9	27.3	24.2	24.9	26.1	24.6
AW,HL	28.6	28.0	24.9	26.0	26.1	26.0	24.3	25.4	25.5	24.9	25.0	25.6	27.0	27.4	24.2	25.1	26.2	24.7
AW,AW	28.6	28.0	25.0	26.3	26.4	26.2	24.3	25.6	25.6	25.2	25.3	25.8	27.0	27.4	24.3	25.4	26.5	24.9
AW,AD	28.3	27.6	24.5	25.1	25.1	25.0	24.1	25.1	25.2	24.0	24.0	24.7	26.7	27.1	24.0	24.2	25.3	23.9
AW,AL	28.4	27.8	25.4	26.5	26.5	26.4	24.6	25.7	25.8	25.8	25.9	26.2	26.9	27.4	24.5	25.9	26.6	25.6
AD,BW	28.3	27.7	25.5	26.5	26.5	26.4	24.7	25.9	25.9	26.0	26.3	26.9	27.3	24.7	25.9	26.6	25.7	
AD,BD	29.0	28.7	26.0	28.4	28.4	28.2	24.9	26.3	26.4	27.5	27.5	27.9	27.3	27.9	24.8	27.4	28.4	26.8
AD,HL	29.2	28.9	25.9	28.8	28.8	28.6	24.9	26.4	26.5	27.7	27.8	28.2	27.3	28.0	24.8	27.7	28.8	26.9
AD,AW	28.4	27.8	24.8	25.8	25.8	25.6	24.2	25.4	25.4	24.7	24.8	25.3	26.9	27.3	24.2	24.9	26.0	24.5
AD,AD	28.5	27.8	25.0	26.1	26.0	25.9	24.3	25.5	25.5	25.1	25.1	25.6	26.9	27.3	24.2	25.2	26.3	24.8
AD,AL	28.5	28.0	25.8	27.1	27.2	27.1	25.0	26.2	26.2	26.6	26.7	26.9	27.1	27.5	24.9	26.6	27.2	26.3
AL,BW	28.4	28.2	26.4	27.6	27.6	27.6	25.5	26.6	26.7	27.3	27.2	27.4	27.2	27.7	25.4	27.2	27.6	27.0
AL,BD	29.6	29.5	27.4	30.1	30.1	30.0	25.9	27.6	27.6	29.5	29.5	29.7	27.8	28.6	25.9	29.4	30.0	28.9
AL,HL	28.9	28.7	26.4	28.3	28.3	28.2	25.4	26.7	26.8	27.8	27.8	27.9	27.4	27.9	25.2	27.7	28.3	27.2
AL,AW	28.2	27.6	25.0	25.9	25.9	25.8	24.4	25.5	25.6	25.2	25.3	25.6	26.9	27.2	24.4	25.3	26.0	25.0
AL,AD	28.1	27.6	25.2	26.1	26.1	26.1	24.5	25.6	25.6	25.5	25.5	25.9	26.9	27.1	24.5	25.5	26.2	25.3
AL,AL	28.6	28.4	26.8	28.0	28.0	28.0	25.8	27.0	27.0	27.7	27.7	27.8	27.4	27.8	25.7	27.7	28.1	27.4

32

joint frequency tables, to which you can refer and make your results forecasts. These are the tables in figures 13 to 15.

As you use this data remember that the *most recent* result of the home team is the one to the *right* in the 'home dyad' column, while the *last* result of the away team is in the *lower* of the two in the two rows comprising the 'away dyad'.

It is also important to be aware of the *average expectations* of a home win, draw and away win. These are, respectively, **47.5%**, **27.0%** and **25.5%**.

As an example, assume that the last two matches played by opposing teams, for which the next result is to be predicted, ended as follows ....

Home team		Away team
(Dyad)		(Dyad)
HW, AD	vs	AW, HL

To discover the probability of this match being a *home win* find the position on the 'Home Win Probability' table (figure 13) where the *row* of the home dyad **HW,AD** intersects the *column* of the away dyad **AW,HL**. This gives a value **51.2%**, and suggests a *higher than average* expectation of a home.

Next look at the corresponding point of intersection on the 'Away Win Probability' and 'Draw Probability' tables (figures 14 and 15) and read off the respective chances of an away win or draw. You will find that the sum of the three probabilities totals 100%. Compare the probabilities from the tables with the chance expectations listed above. Those which most exceed the average levels are the best rated or 'banker' forecasts.

The mass of data accumulated here necessitated the use of a computer, however the values listed in figures 11 and 12 are in themselves informative, and you may decide to devise and test some simple forecasting rules based upon this information.

Goals Scored

The record of past scores provides many forecasting options.

The intuitive approach is to combine, by means of a simple formula, totals of goals scored and lost by the opposing teams. Here is an example of how this can be achieved. By the way, the abbreviations used below, and throughout this section, are .... HT=home team, AT=away team, GS=goals scored and GL=goals lost.

Home Goal
Points *(HGpts)* = HT,GS + AT,GL

Away Goal
Points *(AGpts)* = HT,GL + AT,GS

Goal Points Diference *(GPD)* = HGpts *minus* AGpts

HOME WIN SCORE PREDICTION

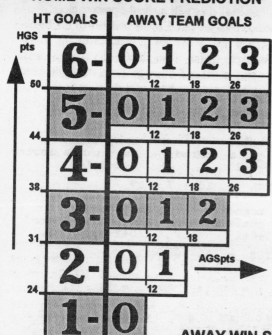

Score Prediction heuristic using the results of the last 5 home matches and last 5 away matches of opposing teams - figure 16

DRAW SCORE PREDICTION

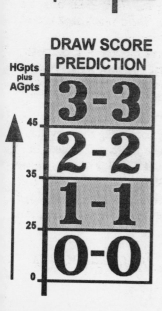

AWAY WIN SCORE PREDICTION

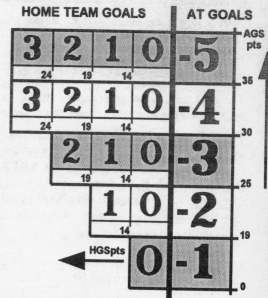

Substituting 'real' data will make the process clear.
This method uses the last 5 home matches of the home team and the last 5 five away matches of the away team. For every match score shown, the home scored goals are on the left and away goals on the right. The most recently played matches are to the right ....

```
home team = 0-2  4-0  0-1  4-1  2-1
away team = 0-1  3-0  3-2  1-0  0-3

Home Goal = home team,          +    away team,
Points      home goals scored        away goals lost
            0+4+0+4+2           +    0+3+3+1+0

HGpts = HTGS + ATGL  =  10 + 7 = 17

Away Goal = home team,     +    away team,
Points      home goals lost     away goals scored
            2+0+1+1+1       +    1+0+2+0+3

AGpts = HTGL + ATGS  =  5 + 6 = 11

Goal Points
Difference ( GPD ) = HGpts - AGpts = 17 - 11 = +6
```

The goal points difference can now be used to categorise predictions as homes draws and aways. A selection of parameter values along the following lines produces reasonable proportions of each category ....

```
GPD = +2 or more    =   Home Win
GPD = -2 or less    =   Away Win
GPD = +1, 0 or -1   =   Draw
```

It can be seen that, with a GPD of +6, the forecast is a *HOME WIN*.

The next step, although fraught with difficulties, is to attempt to use both the GPD and scoring record to predict match scores !

The method tried out here is best understood by continuing the previous example. The GPD was 6, a home win, so the table which will be used in figure 16, is headed '**HOME WIN SCORE PREDICTION**'.

But first calculate **Home Goal Score Points (HGSpts)**.

To the previously calculated Home Goal Points add all goals *scored* by the home team and *lost* by the away team, of 3 or more ....

```
HGSpts = 17 (HGpts) + 4 + 4 + 3 + 3 = 31
```

Under 'HT GOALS' *(the vertical scale, on the left of the 'HOME WIN' table)* find the position where HGSpts = 31.

Read off the **Home Goals** prediction ..... which is **3**.

Note that if the HGSpts value had been less than 31, but greater than or equal to 24, the home goal score prediction would have been 2.

The next requirement is to find the away goals scored forecast, under the 'AWAY TEAM GOALS' heading.
First calculate **Away Goal Score Points (AGSpts)**.
To do so, add, to the previously calculated Away Goal Points, all goals of 3 or more *lost* by the home team and *scored* by the away team ....

```
AGSpts = 11 (AGpts) + 3 = 14
```

On the *horizontal* AGSpts scale, adjacent to the **3** 'HT GOALS' just calculated, locate the approximate position of the value 14. Read off the *Away Goals* prediction which corresponds to this value ... which is **1**.

The score prediction for this HOME WIN is therefore 3-1.

In figure 17 a series of score predictions has been made. You will see that the first and second matches have been predicted, respectively, as 2-4 away win and a 1-1 draw. The relevant calculations are summarised overleaf.

Score prediction examples - figure 17

SCORE PREDICTIONS

pred. score	HGS pts	AGS pts	GPD	HG pts	AG pts	home team, home record	away team, away record
A 2-4	20	30	-3	14	17	3-0 1-0 1-4 0-0 3-2	1-3 2-3 1-1 2-3 0-1
D 1-1	n/a	n/a	0	13	13	2-3 1-3 1-1 1-0 2-0	0-3 2-0 0-1 0-0 4-2
H 3-2	32	25	4	19	15	1-1 0-3 0-1 2-3 0-4	2-0 3-1 6-1 4-1 1-0
A 0-1	6	18	-5	6	11	0-1 0-1 0-0 1-0 1-0	1-1 0-3 2-0 1-4 0-1
H 1-0	12	12	3	12	9	2-1 2-0 1-0 1-1 0-1	1-0 2-2 1-3 2-1 0-0
H 2-1	20	14	10	20	10	3-1 2-0 6-1 2-1 1-0	1-1 2-1 2-4 0-0 1-1
D 2-2	n/a	n/a	1	18	17	1-1 3-2 3-0 3-2 4-1	2-3 0-0 1-4 1-0 0-4
H 3-1	33	13	9	19	10	1-0 0-0 1-3 2-0 0-1	3-0 5-2 3-2 1-0 3-2
A 0-2	11	23	-2	11	13	1-3 2-1 1-1 1-4 0-0	1-3 0-1 1-0 2-0 2-0
H 1-0	18	5	8	13	5	2-0 2-2 1-1 1-0 0-0	0-0 1-0 0-1 5-0 1-1
D 1-1	n/a	n/a	-1	16	17	0-0 2-0 3-1 2-2 1-4	0-1 2-2 1-3 2-3 3-1
D 1-1	n/a	n/a	-1	12	13	1-1 0-1 1-1 1-1 2-1	2-2 0-2 1-1 2-2 2-1
A 1-2	22	20	-2	14	16	1-1 0-1 1-2 0-2 3-2	2-0 0-2 1-1 5-1 1-4
D 1-1	n/a	n/a	1	16	15	1-2 0-2 1-1 3-2 3-1	2-2 1-2 1-1 1-0 3-2
D 1-1	n/a	n/a	0	15	15	1-5 1-2 0-1 2-2 1-1	3-1 1-1 2-1 4-1 0-0
H 2-1	25	16	6	19	13	3-1 1-1 2-1 2-2 2-2	1-3 2-0 3-0 2-2 1-1
H 3-0	31	5	15	20	5	1-0 4-2 2-0 1-0 4-2	3-0 2-0 1-1 1-0 1-0

n/a = not applicable (draw forecast)

In the first game in figure 17 ....
```
HGpts = 3+1+1+0+3 + 1+2+1+2+0 = 14
AGpts = 0+0+4+0+2 + 3+3+1+3+1 = 17
GPD = HGpts-AGpts = 14-17 = -3
```
The prediction is therefore an **AWAY WIN**.

Next calculate the value of AGSpts and find its position on the vertical scale in the table headed 'AWAY WIN SCORE PREDICTION'.

`AGSpts=17(AGpts)+4+3+3+3=30`, and the away goals forecast = **4**

Now find HGSpts on the horizontal scale.

`HGSpts=14(HGpts)+3+3=20`.   The home goals prediction = **2**

The AWAY WIN Score Prediction is therefore 2-4.

The second match in figure 17 is forecast as a draw ....
```
HGpts = 2+1+1+1+2 + 0+2+0+0+4 = 13
AGpts = 3+3+1+0+0 + 3+0+1+0+2 = 13
GPD = HGpts-AGpts = 13-13 = 0
```
This confirms the prediction as a **DRAW**.

In the case of a draw, add together *only* the values HGpts and AGpts.
```
HGpts + AGpts = 13 + 13 = 26
```
From the 'DRAW SCORE PREDICTION TABLE' read the score forecast.
It is a 1-1 DRAW prediction.

There can be no extravagant claims of success for score prediction.

The problem is that there are just too many possible outcomes for each game (take a glance at figure 18). Using the approach just described matches can be forecast as homes, draws and aways with some reliability, however the score forecast can be regarded as no more than a guide to the goal scoring potential, and defensive ability, of the opposing teams.

There are of course other ways to use 'goal data' to make results forecasts. For example *goal averages* per game could be calculated for opposing teams and the values compared. Alternatively the 'goal difference' commonly listed in football league tables might be adapted for predictive purposes.

All in all, the use of goals scored as a forecasting criterion seems to have considerable merit and must be worthy of further investigation.

FORECASTING SUMMARISED
The preceding pages will have left the reader in no doubt of the mass of information available for collation and processing. In fact statistical data can be conveniently divided into two categories, descriptive and inferential. You may decide to collect data which serves only a descriptive purpose.

The information is presented in such a way as to summarise or accentuate important features, but goes no further. Tables of league points, or goals scored, fall into this category. Statistics of this sort may nevertheless influence your betting decisions and can generate new ideas.

Consider figure 18. The tables cover English league games and show the numbers and proportions of scores of each kind over five consecutive football seasons. Some of the values may surprise you ....

1. The most common of all match results is the 1-1 draw.

2. The likeliest home wins *and* away wins are 1-0 victories, accounting, respectively, for 10.8% and 7.4% of games played.

3. 19% of matches end up as a score draw (1-1, 2-2, etc). This is, on average, 11 of the 58 pools coupon matches.

4. The six most prevalent match scores, totalling well over half of the games played, are ... 1-1, 1-0, 2-1, 2-0, 0-0 and 0-1.

5. Only 22 matches, of the 10,148 analysed in the preparation of this table, were games in which a team scored 7 or more goals.

Data such as this is of particular interest to the fixed-odds punter, especially if attempting correct score prediction.

Another example of descriptive material is provided in figure 19. This data emphasises the need to keep an eye open for those 'exceptions to the rule' which come to light from time to time when football records are analysed.

The table shows the proportions of home wins, draws and away wins for the major English and Scottish league divisions during season 1994-95. You will notice the high incidence of home wins in the English First Division, and the small proportion of draws and many aways in the Scottish Third. Also note the variability when the average numbers of goals scored in each division are compared.

Such information may influence your betting selections.... but to what are these differences attributable, and will the trends continue in the future as they have in the past ? In short, are such statistics of predictive value ?

Statistics can certainly be used to make inferences which go beyond the obvious facts. Inferential statistics require that a sample of data is analysed in the hope that conclusions can be drawn on the behaviour of a whole 'population'. This is more to our purpose. If the data is carefully gathered and correctly interpreted this may lead to the development of an original betting strategy or winning system. The previously described 'triad' predictions are based upon statistics of this type.

Number and Percentage of Goals Scored by teams in the major English league divisions for seasons 1990-91 to 1994-95 (10,126 games) - figure 18

NUMBER OF SCORES OF EACH KIND

	away goals scored						
home goals scored	0	1	2	3	4	5	6
0	829	752	398	142	47	10	1
1	1094	1293	676	247	52	17	3
2	842	955	501	172	47	19	2
3	439	455	268	118	33	3	2
4	157	171	99	55	11	3	4
5	50	61	39	12	5	1	0
6	11	13	15	2	0	0	0

PERCENTAGE OF SCORES

	away goals scored						
home goals scored	0	1	2	3	4	5	6
0	8.18	7.42	3.93	1.40	0.46	0.09	0.01
1	10.80	12.77	6.67	2.44	0.50	0.16	0.03
2	8.31	9.43	4.94	1.70	0.46	0.18	0.02
3	4.33	4.49	2.64	1.16	0.32	0.03	0.02
4	1.55	1.68	0.97	0.54	0.10	0.03	0.04
5	0.49	0.60	0.38	0.11	0.05	0.01	0.00
6	0.10	0.12	0.14	0.02	0.00	0.00	0.00

**Variation in proportions of
results and goals scored
- figure 19**

**Proportions of Homes, Draws and Aways, and
Home & Away Goal Averages for Season 1994-95**
(ranked in descending order)

HOME wins%	DRAWN games%	AWAY wins%	HOME Goal (ave.)	AWAY Goal (ave.)
Eng-1 49.64	Sco-P 32.78	Sco-3 41.67	Eng-3 1.53	Sco-3 1.43
Eng-2 45.65	Eng-P 29.00	Sco-1 28.89	Eng-1 1.52	Eng-3 1.13
Sco-2 45.56	Sco-1 28.89	Sco-2 28.82	Eng-P 1.51	Eng-2 1.12
Eng-3 45.24	Eng-1 27.90	Eng-3 28.57	Sco-2 1.51	Sco-1 1.12
Eng-P 44.37	Eng-2 26.99	Eng-2 27.36	Eng-2 1.49	Sco-2 1.11
Sco-P 42.22	Eng-3 26.19	Eng-P 26.63	Sco-3 1.49	Eng-P 1.08
Sco-1 42.22	Sco-2 25.56	Sco-P 25.00	Sco-P 1.47	Sco-1 1.04
Sco-3 41.11	Sco-3 17.22	Eng-1 22.46	Sco-1 1.41	Eng-1 1.00

Averages for all matches (1994-95) ...
Home Wins = 45.5%   Draws = 27.0%   Away Wins = 27.5%
Home Goals Scored = 1.5   Away Goals Scored = 1.1

In general, the nature of a set of data will do much to suggest the use to which it can be put. Even so, there are invariably a number of difficult arbitrary decisions to be made. For example, if sequences of results are to be analysed, how many matches should be included, and are home and away sequences to be considered independently ? The forecaster must also decide how the various parameters should be set which categorise results, and the numerical values which are to be placed upon factors like home advantage or league division status.

It is important to carry out regular statistical analyses of prediction successes *(or 'strike rates' as they are often called)*. In doing so you may find that certain strategies are less reliable at the start or close of a football season, and could decide to regulate your approach to selection and staking accordingly. It is also possible that different methods may produce similar *overall* levels of success, although the individual predictions for the same set of matches may differ quite markedly.

There is no doubt that the compilation, interpretation and use of statistics requires considerable care. There are 'good' and 'bad' statistics, and it is not unknown for entirely erroneous conclusions to be derived from sound data.

Draws on the pools coupon lines - figure 20

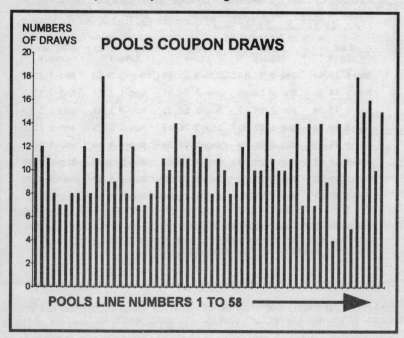

This is the case in the next example. In figure 20 the histogram shows the numbers of draws occurring against each pools coupon match line number over a single British football season. Thus, in the first match line, 11 games ended as draws, in the second line there were 12 draws, and so on.

The misuse of data such as this invariably indicates a lack of understanding of the fundamentals of probability. You will find that these statistics are made to make draw selections in the mistaken belief that, because there have been many draws in certain coupon lines in the past, these same lines should be avoided in the future. Alternatively, it is sometimes argued that where few draws have occurred in a match line they must be imminent. Such interpretations are ill-founded.

Misconceptions of this kind are common in both sports betting and games of pure chance, such as the lottery.

The term 'Monte Carlo Fallacy' has been applied.

Consider the toss of a coin. The chance of tossing a head *at one attempt* is widely known to be one in two. It is less well accepted that the probability of tossing a sixth head, *after* five consecutive heads have been thrown, is also one in two. This is very different from the probability of throwing six heads in a row, as calculated *before* the first of the six throws is made. The chance of throwing six consecutive heads, *as assessed before the very first throw,* is one in sixtyfour....

1/2 X 1/2 X 1/2 X 1/2 X 1/2 X 1/2 = 1/64

The confusion lies in not distinguishing the difference between the probability of a single event and that of a series of events *before* the occurrence of the first event in the series.

The part of *Football Fortunes* dealing with probabilities will help make this distinction clear, but for the time being it should be remembered that the chance of a draw appearing against a match line on a pools coupon is not determined by the previous occurrence of draws in that same line. *

Similarly, winning lottery numbers *cannot* be forecast by analysing the frequency of the occurrence of past numbers. Such analyses, which appear regularly in magazines and newspapers, have an aura of pseudo-scientific authority but in truth are a waste of time, effort and paper.

Regrettably some pools companies are guilty of perpetuating this myth by publishing statistics showing the distribution of draws on pools coupons throughout the football season, and even go so far as to openly advise that the information be used to make your treble chance selections !

The sporting press print many statistics of a similar nature, and of equally dubious value. You will read that one team has played 12 matches without a defeat, or another has gone 7 games and is yet to win. Be careful about the conclusions you draw from such information.

A final word. It should be borne in mind that although statistical tables and prediction algorithms may provide a very valuable guide to your selections, the betting strategy you choose is equally important in terms of overall success and the return on your wagers. You will find that much of the remainder of this book is devoted to this very subject.

* Note : The possible exception might be when matches from certain league divisions, in which the distribution of draws is considerably more or less than the average, appear regularly against the same coupon line numbers (see figure 19).

Football Pools Betting

John Moores launched the first football 'pools' enterprise from a small office in Liverpool in 1922. It began with a total capital of £150. The business started badly, and two of Moores' original partners, one of whom was named *Littlewood* (and after whom the company was named) decided to quit the venture. However by the end of the 1926-27 football season the business began to thrive. Other companies became established, and the pools have become a way of life in the United Kingdom ever since.

Like the bookmaker, the pools companies have had to fight considerable Government antagonism, vociferously supported by anti-gambling MP's. In addition they have faced, until recently at least, opposition from the football authorities, who feared a threat to true competition and the 'good name' of football. Indeed, so great was the hostility that the football league at one stage attempted to withold the match fixtures until two days before kick-off. This sparked off a 'pools war' which was not resolved until 1958.

The response of the pools companies to this open aggression was the formation, in 1934, of the Pools Promoters Association (PPA). The organisation continues to this day, despite the much improved relationship with both Government and football authorities..... a relationship improved, in no small part, by the regular receipt of a cut of the staked pools money !

In 1995, concerned about the impact of the lottery, pools companies were able to obtain various concessions from the Government. The £2.25 million ceiling on a single prize was removed, roll-over jackpots were allowed, and rules were relaxed on advertising. In 1995, and again in 1996, the tax on pools was reduced. Such reforms were long overdue. The pools companies have also introduced new pools 'cards', comparable to those used for the lottery. These are computer-readable and easier to complete.

The football 'pools' themselves, like the lottery, are a form of *pari-mutuel* betting. All of the money staked is placed in the pool. The organisers (and as we have seen various others) take their share, before the remainder is divided amongst the winners. The consequence is that less than 30% of the stake money is returned to the gambler.

This form of gambling means that, unlike placing a bet with a bookmaker, the return on the investment is *not* known in advance. In fact it is impossible to assess the monetary return, not only because the total number of participants is unknown, but because there can be several winners with the same correct winning forecast. In such circumstances the top prize is shared.

The principal attractions of the pools seem to be the application of 'skill and judgement' to the prediction of results and the lure of the potentially huge prizes.

Up until the 1940s the 'Penny Points' coupon (so called because each line on the coupon cost a penny) was the most popular kind of pool's entry. However the **'Treble Chance'** football pool was introduced in 1946, and now accounts for the vast majority of the money staked, although there are *minor* pools for home wins, away wins and draws.

The pools are able to operate all year round by making use of both British and Australian football matches.

There are currently some 10 million people playing the pools each week in the United Kingdom, and around £15 million is spent by the public on the search for those elusive football matches which will result in a draw.

POOLS ENTRIES

A pool of prize money is certainly shared amongst the winners, although the term 'treble chance' has become a misnomer. So called because of the three possible outcomes of a game (home win, away win or draw), there are now four categories. Draws may be 'score' or 'no-score'.

The object is to identify, from the total number of matches listed on a pools coupon, **eight score draws**. A score draw is, appropriately enough, any drawn game in which goals are scored (1-1, 2-2, 3-3, etc).

Eight correctly forecast score draws give the top prize, the **1st Dividend**; although all pools companies offer several additional, lesser, dividends. *The dividend you receive depends upon points gained.*

Each category of match result is allocated points as follows ....

```
Score Draw (1-1, 2-2, etc ) ........... 3pts
No Score Draw ( 0-0 ) or Void match ... 2pts
Home win or Away win ................. 1pt
```

An extract from a pools coupon appears in figure 21. Note that individual matches on the coupon are identified by a number, and there is a series of columns, headed A, B, C, etc, where your draw selections are placed.

Unless pools 'plans' are being used *(page 48)*, you can be sure that if any one column of your selections on the coupon contains *eight* correctly forecast score draws, it is worth **24pts**, and wins a 1st dividend. There may be dividends for smaller points totals (23, 22, 21, etc), although the payout will vary with the pools company. The return also depends upon the total number of matches listed on the coupon which end up as draws.

To fill in a coupon decide upon the type of entry to be submitted (*more on this shortly*) and mark an **'X'** against potential score draws. In doing so, care must be taken to avoid *cancelled matches* which will *not* be dealt with by the 'pools panel' (see page 53). These will be declared 'void', and are worth only 2 points. Check newspapers and television during the days preceding the

Extract from a pools coupon - figure 21

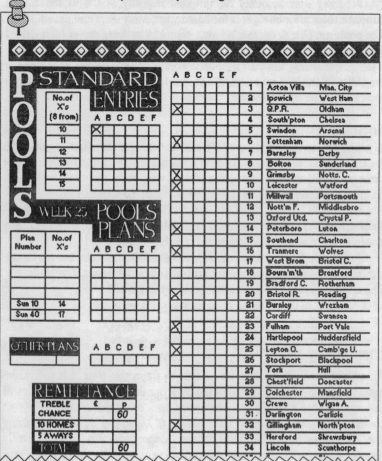

No.	Home	Away
1	Aston Villa	Man. City
2	Ipswich	West Ham
3	Q.P.R.	Oldham
4	South'pton	Chelsea
5	Swindon	Arsenal
6	Tottenham	Norwich
7	Barnsley	Derby
8	Bolton	Sunderland
9	Grimsby	Notts. C.
10	Leicester	Watford
11	Millwall	Portsmouth
12	Nott'm F.	Middlesbro
13	Oxford Utd.	Crystal P.
14	Peterboro	Luton
15	Southend	Charlton
16	Tranmere	Wolves
17	West Brom	Bristol C.
18	Bourn'm'th	Brentford
19	Bradford C.	Rotherham
20	Bristol R.	Reading
21	Burnley	Wrexham
22	Cardiff	Swansea
23	Fulham	Port Vale
24	Hartlepool	Huddersfield
25	Leyton O.	Camb'ge U.
26	Stockport	Blackpool
27	York	Hull
28	Chest'field	Doncaster
29	Colchester	Mansfield
30	Crewe	Wigan A.
31	Darlington	Carlisle
32	Gillingham	North'pton
33	Hereford	Shrewsbury
34	Lincoln	Scunthorpe

STANDARD ENTRIES

No. of X's (8 from)	A	B	C	D	E	F
10						
11						
12						
13						
14						
15						

WEEK 25 — POOLS PLANS

Plan Number	No. of X's	A	B	C	D	E	F
Sun 10	14						
Sun 40	17						

OTHER PLANS

	A	B	C	D	E	F

REMITTANCE

	£	p
TREBLE CHANCE		60
10 HOMES		
5 AWAYS		
TOTAL		60

fixture date to find void matches.
The *total number* of X's which can be placed in any one column (in which

you are trying to trap eight score draws) is determined by the type of pools entry you wish to submit. For example, your selections may often take the form of a straight, or full 'permutation'. *This means that you will be selecting more than eight matches in a single column of the coupon.* Full cover perms are the most

popular kind of pools entry. They are easy to enter, simple to check, and offer many winning chances. Consider the full perm in figure 21. Ten matches have been marked 'X', as score draw forecasts. This allows a large number of entries of eight selections to be submitted, when it would be an impracticable task to write out each of the entries individually. For example, the comparatively small perm of 8 from 10 gives a total of 45 winning chances. As the size of the permutation increases so too does the number of entries and, of course, the total cost of the bet. See figure 22.

Perms of 8 from:	number of lines of 8 entailed:
9	9
10	45
11	165
12	495
13	1,287
14	3,003
15	6,435
16	12,870
17	24,310
18	43,758
19	75,582
20	125,970
30	5,852,924

Full perms of 8 matches - figure 22

It can be seen that a full perm which consists of 15 draw selections would provide 6,435 *lines* of eight draws. *Note the terminology ! Each 'bet' of eight draw forecasts is traditionally referred to as a 'line'; while each full permutation appears as one column of 'selections' on the pools coupon.*

Full perm checking chart for 8 from 10 selections - figure 23

NO.OF MATCHES GAINING...			YOU HAVE THE SHOWN NUMBER OF LINES WITH THE FOLLOWING POINTS TOTAL...							
3 pts	2 pts	1 pt	24 pts	23 pts	22 pts	21 pts	20 pts	19 pts	18 pts	17 pts
10	-	-	45	-	-	-	-	-	-	-
9	1	-	9	36	-	-	-	-	-	-
9	-	1	9	-	36	-	-	-	-	-
8	2	-	1	16	28	-	-	-	-	-
8	1	1	1	8	8	28	-	-	-	-
8	-	2	1	-	16	-	28	-	-	-
7	3	-	-	3	21	21	-	-	-	-
7	2	1	-	2	8	14	21	-	-	-
7	1	2	-	1	2	14	7	21	-	-
7	-	3	-	-	3	-	21	-	21	-
6	4	-	-	-	6	24	15	-	-	-
6	3	1	-	-	3	9	18	15	-	-
6	2	2	-	-	1	4	13	12	15	-
6	1	3	-	-	-	3	3	18	6	15
6	-	4	-	-	-	-	6	-	24	-
5	5	-	-	-	-	10	25	10	-	-
5	4	1	-	-	-	4	11	20	10	-
5	3	2	-	-	-	1	6	13	15	10
5	2	3	-	-	-	-	3	6	16	10
5	1	4	-	-	-	-	-	6	4	20
5	-	5	-	-	-	-	-	-	10	-
4	6	-	-	-	-	-	15	24	6	-
4	5	1	-	-	-	-	5	14	20	6
4	4	2	-	-	-	-	1	8	14	16
4	3	3	-	-	-	-	-	3	9	15
4	2	4	-	-	-	-	-	-	6	8
4	1	5	-	-	-	-	-	-	-	10
3	7	-	-	-	-	-	-	21	21	3
3	6	1	-	-	-	-	-	6	18	18
3	5	2	-	-	-	-	-	1	10	16
3	4	3	-	-	-	-	-	-	3	12
3	3	4	-	-	-	-	-	-	-	6
2	8	-	-	-	-	-	-	-	28	16
2	7	1	-	-	-	-	-	-	7	23
2	6	2	-	-	-	-	-	-	1	12
2	5	3	-	-	-	-	-	-	-	3
1	9	-	-	-	-	-	-	-	-	36
1	8	1	-	-	-	-	-	-	-	8
1	7	2	-	-	-	-	-	-	-	1

Full perm checking chart
for 8 from 11 selections
- figure 24

47

NO.OF MATCHES GAINING...			YOU HAVE THE SHOWN NUMBER OF LINES WITH THE FOLLOWING POINTS TOTAL...						
3 pts	2 pts	1 pt	24 pts	23 pts	22 pts	21 pts	20 pts	19 pts	18 pts
11	-	-	165	-	-	-	-	-	-
10	1	-	45	120	-	-	-	-	-
10	-	1	45	-	120	-	-	-	-
9	2	-	9	72	84	-	-	-	-
9	1	1	9	36	36	84	-	-	-
9	-	2	9	-	72	-	84	-	-
8	3	-	1	24	84	56	-	-	-
8	2	1	1	16	36	56	21	-	-
8	1	2	1	8	16	56	28	56	-
8	-	3	1	-	24	-	84	-	56
7	4	-	-	4	42	84	35	-	-
7	3	1	-	3	22	42	63	35	-
7	2	2	-	2	9	28	49	42	35
7	1	3	-	1	3	21	21	63	21
7	-	4	-	-	4	-	42	-	84
6	5	-	-	-	10	60	75	20	-
6	4	1	-	-	6	28	51	60	20
6	3	2	-	-	3	12	37	48	45
6	2	3	-	-	1	6	21	36	51
6	1	4	-	-	-	4	6	36	24
6	-	5	-	-	-	-	10	-	60
5	6	-	-	-	-	20	75	60	10
5	5	1	-	-	-	10	35	60	50
5	4	2	-	-	-	4	17	44	50
5	3	3	-	-	-	1	9	24	46
5	2	4	-	-	-	-	4	12	34
5	1	5	-	-	-	-	-	10	10
5	-	6	-	-	-	-	-	-	20
4	7	-	-	-	-	-	35	84	42
4	6	1	-	-	-	-	15	44	66
4	5	2	-	-	-	-	5	24	50
4	4	3	-	-	-	-	1	12	30
4	3	4	-	-	-	-	-	4	18
4	2	5	-	-	-	-	-	-	10
3	8	-	-	-	-	-	-	56	84
3	7	1	-	-	-	-	-	21	56
3	6	2	-	-	-	-	-	6	33
3	5	3	-	-	-	-	-	1	15
3	4	4	-	-	-	-	-	-	4
2	9	-	-	-	-	-	-	-	84
2	8	1	-	-	-	-	-	-	28
2	7	2	-	-	-	-	-	-	7
2	6	3	-	-	-	-	-	-	1

To complete a pools coupon, make your score draw forecasts and place an 'X' in one of the 'entry' boxes to indicate your choice of plan or permutation (*the perm is 8 from 10 in figure 21*). You will also have to enter the total cost of your bet, your name, address and telephone number. You must of course enclose a cheque or postal order to pay for your wager. If you do not want details of winnings to be publicised, place an 'X' in the 'no publicity' box.

The pools companies provide a 'copy coupon' for your retention. Use this to record details of your entry and to check match results. There will also be a unique coupon reference number which should be quoted if you make a claim for a prize or have enquiries of any kind. The pools companies generally ask that you submit a claim for a 24 point line if there are eleven or less score draws on the copon. There are various telephone services, including 'freephone' help lines, to deal with your queries.

Match results appear on Saturday evening on TV, Teletext and radio, and are comprehensively covered in the Sunday newspapers. When it comes to checking your coupon, it is important to realise that you do not add together the points gained by *all* of your selections in one column, but only the *best* 8. The 8 from 10 perm guarantees a first dividend if you have correctly predicted eight score draws out of the ten selected. With less than eight correct draws correct you might still win a prize. For example the highest number of points achieved might be for six score draws, one no-score draw, and one home win. This gives a total of 21 points.

In fact with a full cover perm there is always the chance of winning *more than one* dividend. If you use full perms of 8 from 10, or 11, then the checking charts in figures 23 and 24 should be consulted to determine the total number of dividends of each kind you have won.

Full details of dividend payouts are available from around mid-day on the Wednesday following the matches. Check newspapers and Teletext.

Returning to the completion of the coupon itself. *It is important not to confuse the full cover perm with the 'pools plan'.* Pools plans keep down the total cost of a pools entry by reducing the number of lines submitted. This works as follows. If you were to make 20 draw selections a full cover permutation (ie 8 from 20) would consist of 125,970 lines. The cost does of course vary from one pools company to another, but such a large number of lines is not going to come cheaply. A typical pools plan attempts to *reduce* the total number of lines by discarding those combinations of match selections which are thought 'unlikely' to occur. For example, it might perhaps be argued that correct draw selections rarely fall consecutively, and so should not be included in your pools entry.

There can be no doubt that pools plans which adopt such methods cut down upon the total number of lines submitted; but it can reasonably be argued that this is simply at the expense of winning chances. This is an important point which will be pursued a little later.

However, for the moment, it is sufficient to note that of the various pools plans available many carry a useful 'guarantee'. Typically this might be that with 9 correctly forecast score draws amongst your 16 selections, *at least* 7 score draws will fall together, providing a minimum dividend of 22 points. The benefit of such a plan is that, with the stated number of correct score forecasts (in this case 9) you are immediately aware that you have obtained at least the minimum guaranteed points total.

Many of the most popular plans have been prepared by the pools companies and newspapers. The plan just mentioned, with the '7 if 9' guarantee, is *Vernon's* 'V PLAN 43' and consists of 180 lines

Extremely popular, is the 'Sun Plan 40'. This was devised in the 1960s and covers 17 selections in 600 lines. If any eight score draws occur in these 17 selections then it is guaranteed that 7 will fall together and you are assured of at least 22 points *(7 X 3 = 21, plus at least 1 more point)*. Full cover would require 24,310 lines, so the saving in cost is considerable. However it must be borne in mind that winning chances are being reduced.... in this case by a factor of 40 !

It is simple enough to submit a pools plan. In one column of your coupon mark the appropriate number of 'X's, as score draw predictions for the plan you have chosen, and place an 'X' against the name of the chosen plan.

Although a plan guarantee provides a superficial guide to your winnings, to know precisely how many points and dividends have been won a 'checking chart' is a necessity. These charts are set out in columns of eight X's, or consist of blocks producing combinations of X's. You must compare the results of your forecasts with the checking chart for the appropriate plan. The procedure for checking pools plans is described on page 55.

Pools plan checking charts are generally available from the customer services department of the pools companies. There are also computer programs which will quickly check the total points gained.

Finally, examine any pools coupon and it will not escape your notice that there is invariably a provision for the punter to try forecasting home wins and away wins. Such additional betting options on a coupon are sometimes optimistically referred to as 'Bread-and-Butter Pools' !

It may be convenient to include selections of this kind with your treble chance entry but, for a less restrictive wager and a superior return on your investment, fixed-odds betting is to be preferred.

POOLS BETTING STRATEGY

There are the five factors which will dictate your approach to betting on the football pools ....

1. The number of entry lines.
2. The total cost of the bet.
3. The prize money.
4. Type of pools entry.
5. Your forecasting ability.

It is self-evident that the **number of lines** submitted (ie entries of eight score draws) has a fundamental bearing upon the likelihood of success. This is easily demonstrated.

You will doubtless have heard of the astronomical odds against winning the pools. Take the case where *exactly eight* of the 58 matches on a pools coupon end up as scoring draws. The probability of identifying these eight draws with precisely *eight selections* can be calculated without difficulty.

At the first attempt the chance of finding a draw is clearly 8 from 58. On the second attempt there remain 7 unselected draws, from a total number of matches now reduced to 57. So the chance is 7 from 57. The third choice is 6 from 56, and so on. The process continues, and the overall probability can be expressed as follows ...

8/58 X 7/57 X 6/56 X 5/55 X 4/54 X 3/53 X 2/52 X 1/51

Multiply out, and the odds are just short of **1 in 2 billion**.

Nil desperandum. The odds against success fall rapidly as the number of *lines* of eight score draw forecasts increases. For example, if 1000 lines are submitted the odds fall to a mere 2 million to 1 !

Odds improve further still when more of the matches end as score draws. With 12 score draws results, and 1000 lines of eight selections in your entry, the chance of a 1st dividend is approximately 1 in 4000.

The important point to note is that it is the number of coupon lines which is directly under your control, and the more lines submitted the greater the prospects of success.

It is of course all too clear that any increase in the number of lines submitted has a direct consequence upon the second factor which determines your betting strategy..... **the total cost of the bet**.

Thankfully, there are ways to reduce costs, or increase winning chances. One solution is to join (or form) a syndicate. A group's purchasing power is much greater than that of an individual, but be careful, there are a number of potential problems which must be addressed.

To avoid disputes amongst syndicate members it is a good idea to prepare a *syndicate agreement*. This can be laid out as shown ....

> *We the undersigned have agreed to share the*
> *cost of a weekly pools entry on ....*
> *(state pool company)   coupon in the name of*
> *......................... (state organiser's name) and*
> *to share any winnings in respect thereof in the*
> *following proportions ....*
> *(list name and percentage share of each member).*

Group members can act as witnesses, and all members should have a copy. It may be advisable to add a clause to the effect that should any member's payment fall into arrears their membership will lapse. To this end keep accurate records. It is also prudent to include an 'escape clause' in the event of the organiser making an error in completing or submitting a coupon. The pools coupon itself must be submitted in the name of one individual, not that of a syndicate.

Information on this, and much more, is available from the Pools Promoters Association (PPA) at this address...

PPA, c/o Walton Hall Avenue,
LIVERPOOL. L67 1AA
Tel : 0800 500 000

Of course it makes sense to be acquainted with other members of a syndicate, and to feel that they are honest. There was, in September 1994, an instance of a syndicate member pocketing a £30 stake when total winings for the correct coupon entry would have been around £2 million.

It is also advisable to be a little wary of 'commercial' syndicates, and certainly treat with caution promises of massive returns or unrealistic guarantees. Commercial operations generally take a slice of any prizes to cover 'overheads', and, as far as football pools are concerned, could be in breach of the strict laws governing such activities in the United Kingdom.

By far the easiest way to keep down expenses, or to increase your winning chances, is to place your bet with a pools company offering a lower basic charge per entry line. For example the unit cost of *Zetters* is currently one-twelfth that of *Littlewoods*. The drawback is fairly obvious. All wagers are placed in a common pool, so lower stakes also mean smaller dividends. The **prize money** is therefore the third factor you will want to consider when submitting a coupon. You must answer the question.... for the same cost, would you prefer a slim chance of winning £2 million, or perhaps *twelve times* that chance of winnning £75,000 ?

The choice is yours !

Let us assume that you have decided upon the pools company with which you intend to invest; and that you will go for the maximum number of lines you can afford. The next step is to decide upon the **type of entry** you wish to place. You may be inclined to select a full cover permutation. This should certainly be your choice if you believe that, having made your score draw selections, they are all, more or less, *equally likely* to be correct. However, it may be your belief that certain combinations or sequences of selections offer less value than others, and consquently are wasteful of money. If this is your understanding then use a pools plan. For example you might think that there is *little chance* of correct draw selections occurring consecutively, or of only evenly numbered selections being correct, or only odd. If you are convinced that this is a legitimate argument then by all means make use of a pools plan devised to avoid entries which include these, and other, unwanted patterns. *However the statistician would undoubtedly insist that this is not a sound approach and that factors such as these have no bearing upon the distribution of correct draw selections on a coupon.*

Whether your choice be full perm or pools plan, it is clear that your **forecasting abilities** will play a key role in your fortunes. Prediction methods have been discussed extensively in this booklet, and it has been pointed out that, of the three possible outcomes of a game, a draw is invariably the most difficult to predict. In fact you may have read claims that attempts to forecast draws are no better than random selections. This is not true. The software suppliers *'Forth Dimension'* have maintained a

Draw prediction success rates - figure 25

DRAW PREDICTION SUCCESSES   1990 to 1995

Percentage of results which were draws.... 27.20%

Average correct forecasts from all of the weekly draw predictions made....... 29.16%

Average correct forecasts from the 'best eight' weekly draw predictions...... 33.76%

Note : this data refers only to matches which appeared in 'pools coupons' over the stated period.

---

record of forecasting success rates for draws over a five
year period (1990-1995). Their analysis reveals that,
although the gain over chance is not considerable, a
statistically significant improvement can be achieved.
See figure 25. Over the period in question, analysis of
the top-rated weekly draw predictions shows a success

rate some 25% *better* than that which might have been expected by chance.
(The analysis is statistically significant at the p<0.0001 level).

By the way another common misconception is that 'cup' matches are more
likely to result in draws than league games. In fact the proportion of draws,
homes and aways is very similar for both league and cup fixtures.

Here is another misguided selection strategy.

It is difficult enough to forecast draws, so do not be misled by the advice
that, in their selection, an allowance should be made which takes account
of the *random* element. This is the so-called 'unexpected' draw. If such
results *are* truly unexpected then, by definition, they *cannot* be predicted !

Simply be guided by your chosen prediction method, whatever it may be.
There are countless approaches to forecasting, and each will introduce a
considerable element of uncertainty. There is no sense in adding further
uncertainties of your own making by including random selections.

There is some advantage in using a collector service for your coupons, or in
submitting entries with a bookmaker using their computerised cards (see
figure 26). Entries can also be placed over the 'Internet'. If the entry is
submitted by the latest possible deadline, the most recent results and
knowledge can be applied in your deliberations. There is also a greater
chance that any matches which have been declared void since the
preparation of the coupon fixtures can be omitted from your selections.

The keen pools punter may also decide to join up with one of the UK-wide
football 'intelligence' networks whose members share the very latest
information on their local football teams in the hope of establishing an
'edge' over the pools company or bookmaker.

A brief comment concerning a comparatively recent innovation, the **'pools
panel'**. Formed so that severe weather conditions would not disrupt
gambling, *postponed* games which appear on the pools coupon are analysed
by a panel of 'experts' and an adjudication given on the probable result. It
seems that the *current form* of the opposing teams may be the criterion for
their decisions. Perhaps a glut of postponed games could prove
advantageous to those of us who base our forecasts on the analysis of form ?

A final word of advice. Avoid prediction systems which make use of the
'pattern' of past results on the treble chance coupon. The theory is that the
pools is a 'numbers game' and that for predictive purposes the *distribution*

54

of draws on the football coupon should be analysed. To 'help' the punter, pools companies and newspapers provide weekly lists of score draw sequences.

This is a poor strategy, and has much in common to that applied in the *so-called* prediction of lottery numbers (see page 40).

Computerised 'full perm' entry card - figure 26

TREBLE CHANCE ENTRY

MARK LIKE THIS ⊏▭▭⊐

			A	B	C	D	E	F
8 from 10	£1-00	10 selections	☐	☐	☐	☐	☐	☐
8 from 10	75p	10 selections	☐	☐	☐	☐	☐	☐
8 from 10	60p	10 selections	☐	☐	☐	☐	☐	☐
8 from 11	£2-20	11 selections	☐	☐	☐	☐	☐	☐
8 from 12	£6-60	12 selections	☐	☐	☐	☐	☐	☐
8 from 13	£17-16	13 selections	☐	☐	☐	☐	☐	☐

MATCH SELECTIONS

A		B		C		D		E		F	
1	30	1	30	1	30	1	30	1	30	1	30
2	31	2	31	2	31	2	31	2	31	2	31
3	32	3	32	3	32	3	32	3	32	3	32
4	33	4	33	4	33	4	33	4	33	4	33
5	34	5	34	5	34	5	34	5	34	5	34
6	35	6	35	6	35	6	35	6	35	6	35
7	36	7	36	7	36	7	36	7	36	7	36
8	37	8	37	8	37	8	37	8	37	8	37

MATCHES, SELECTIONS and LINES

Here is an explanation for some of the terms associated with the football pools which can cause confusion.

In particular take care not to confuse the **match** number on a pools coupon with the draw **selection** number.

The *match number* (currently no's. 1 to 58) identifies individual soccer games listed on the pools coupon.

The *selection number* can best be seen as the ordinal number of the score draw selection. These are the selections submitted by the punter, and marked 'X' down columns of a pools coupon.

Consider the example in figure 21, where the entry is a full permutation of 8 from 10 selections. In this case *match number* 3 is *selection number* 1, and *match number* 6 is *selection number* 2, and so on.

The terms 'consecutive' and 'non-consecutive' are frequently applied when considering score draw selections. Consecutive *selections* follow in sequence down a column of a pools coupon. In figure 21, draw selections 1 and 2, which are match numbers 3 and 6, are consecutive selections. Again take care to distinguish between match numbers and selection numbers. Only *match numbers* 9 and 10 on the coupon in figure 21, *for which selections have been made,* are consecutive. All of the other matches marked with an 'X' are non-consecutive.

It is also important to be aware of the specialised use of the word 'line'.

Occasionally you may see a *complete column* of selections described as a line. However a line is better regarded as a *single bet* of eight score draw forecasts. So, continuing the above example, a full cover perm of 10 score draw selections, as shown in figure 21, consists of *45 lines*. Similarly a small pools plan might require 16 selections and give the punter 30 lines. It is of course the total number of lines (or bets) which make up each permutation or plan which determines the cost of the pools entry.

It may surprise you that 'lines' often refer to *vertical sets of data,* such as the individual *columns* in a pools plan checking chart.

PLANS, PERMS and BLOCKS
Checking a Pools Plan

It is easy enough to check a full cover permutation. Just count up the number of points your best eight selections have achieved (*as explained on page 48*). However, when it comes to pools plans, the checking process is a little more complex and time-consuming.

Each pools plan has its own 'checking chart' which lists *all* of the lines contained in the plan. Checking charts can be obtained directly from the pools companies.

A simple way to check the number of points you have gained is to prepare a 'template' using paper or thin card. Rule off the card with horizontal lines which correspond in position to those found on the checking chart. So, if the pools plan were to consist of 16 selections, mark off 16 rows, as shown in the first part of figure 27.

Preparation of 'template' and checking a 'pools plan' - figure 27

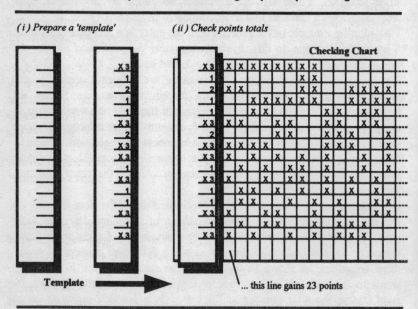

(i) Prepare a 'template'

(ii) Check points totals

Checking Chart

Template ➡

... this line gains 23 points

The next step is to check the match results. Add to the template the points gained for each of your selections in the order in which they appear on the pools coupon. That is, enter '1' point for a home win or away win, '2' for a no-score draw or void match and '3' for a score draw. Of course, generally speaking, unless you have at least 6 correct score draws in your coupon selections there is no need to carry out this check !

It may help you to check through a chart more efficiently if you mark those selections on your template which have gained three points with an 'X', or use some other form of bold indicator.

Place the template against the first column of the chart, align the rows, and begin the checking process *(see part (ii) of figure 27)*. Where there is an 'X' on the checking chart observe the number of points shown on the corresponding row of the template A superficial examination of each line *(ie column)* on the chart will generally be adequate to establish whether you have accumulated sufficient points for a prize. In fact, as you gain practice, a quick glance down each column will be enough to show if you have the minimum requirement of six Xs coinciding across template and chart. If you have achieved this minimum, then count up the *total* points for all eight selections in that particular line. Enter the points total at the foot of the column on the checking chart or simply jot down the number of points gained (and perhaps the column number) on a separate piece of paper. Proceed across the chart until all lines have been checked.

The checking process can be a challenge to the ingenuity of the 'checker'. For example, it is possible to create a template into which holes have been punched corresponding to the location of the score draw results. The template can then be passed quite rapidly across the face of the chart to reveal correct draw forecasts. Other approaches include the use of tracing paper or clear plastic !

The computer user can obtain software which dispenses entirely with this tedious manual checking, and provides points totals at the press of a button.

Guarantee Plans

The most popular of the pools plans are those which provide a 'guarantee'.

The guarantee takes the form that, having achieved the required number of correct score draw predictions, at least one line of the plan will contain a specified number of correct selections.

For example the ever popular 'Sun Plan 40' guarantees that if, out of the 17 score draw forecasts on your coupon, 9 are correct, then you will have at least one plan line containing 7 correct selections. This means that 21 points have been secured, and the points total for that line will depend upon the additional points gained for the eighth match.

The guarantee plan in figure 28 consists of only 30 lines. If there are 8 score draws among the 16 selections there will be at least one line in the plan with 6 score draws. The figure doubles as a checking chart.

Although this plan is simple and inexpensive, it has won fortunes in years past ! However, a 30 line entry provides small coverage, so at the very least, an 8 from 10 full perm, of 45 lines, would seem preferable.

One disadvantage of the pools plans is all too clear. The checking procedure can be extremely laborious. However the guarantee does provide a helpful guide to your winning chances. The great variety of plans available also increase your options when it comes to the number of lines submitted and, consequently, the total amount invested. If you are interested in the construction of 'planned entries' read the explanation on page 108, where guarantee blocks are used in the preparation of fixed-odds coupon entries.

Example of a 'guarantee' plan - figure 28

1	X	X	X	X	X	X	X	X	X	X	X	X	X	X	X	X	X														
2	X	X	X	X	X									X	X							X	X	X	X	X	X	X	X	X
3	X						X	X	X	X				X	X				X	X	X	X	X	X	X	X	X			
4	X										X	X	X	X	X	X			X	X	X	X					X	X	X	X
5	X	X	X					X	X				X	X				X	X					X	X			X	X	
6	X	X	X					X	X				X	X			X	X			X	X			X	X				
7	X				X	X	X	X					X	X			X	X	X			X	X	X				X	X	
8	X				X	X			X	X	X	X					X	X	X			X			X	X	X	X		
9		X			X			X		X		X			X			X		X			X		X			X		X	X
10		X				X			X		X			X			X			X	X			X							X
11			X		X	X				X			X	X			X			X			X				X	X	X		X
12			X		X			X	X				X			X			X			X	X			X	X			X	X
13		X			X	X		X	X			X			X			X	X		X	X				X	X		X	X	X
14		X			X		X	X		X	X			X			X	X	X		X	X				X	X		X	X	X
15		X	X		X			X			X			X			X	X	X		X			X		X	X		X		X
16		X	X			X	X		X			X			X			X	X	X			X		X			X		X	X

Guarantee of 6 correct if 8 score draws in 16 selections. There are 30 lines.

Multiple Permutations

An example will help illustrate how permutations can be combined to create a pools entry.

A full cover perm of 8 from 14 selections consists of 3003 lines. It does depend upon the cost per line, but this *could* be an expensive investment. However, by dividing 14 selections into two columns of 7 selections a considerable reduction in cost can be achieved. In fact the total number of lines is reduced to 1225. The figure 29, shows such a pools entry.

Each of the two columns consists of a permutation of 4 from 7.

A perm of 4 from 7 gives 35 lines. Combining both columns gives a coupon submission of 1225 lines (35 X 35). The coupon has been annotated with a description of the bet.

Take note that in this, and similar entries, it is vital that each match selection appears only once. The same match cannot be selected in more than one column.

TREBLE CHANCE Mark 'X' plus the Plan or Perm details

Perm any 4 Selections from each Column

35 X 35 = 1225 lines

The entry in figure 29 provides a guarantee. At least four correct draw selections in *each* of the two columns and you have 24 points and a 1st dividend.

You may be told that the rationale behind such an entry is that betting lines are omitted which are so improbable as to be valueless. To quote directly from a well known pools pundit.... "punters must be only too aware from their own experiences that whereas 4 correct out of seven selections is exceptionally good picking, the chances of 5, 6 or 7 being correct are so remote that they can be virtually discarded".

Such reasoning does not stand scrutiny.

If it is assumed, for the sake of argument, that all fourteen draw forecasts are equally likely, and eight turn out to be correct, then the correct selections could be *any* of the fourteen. This means that there is a considerable chance that the eight draws will not be distributed in a winning pattern.

With eight correct score draw forecasts in the entry in figure 29 there is a 60% probability that a 1st dividend will *not* be won. For example if 5 score draws occur in the first column and 3 in the second, then your luck is out ! Using this entry, you lose in winning chances what is 'gained' in saved lines.

So disregard claims that you will be getting something for nothing when advised to use a particular permutation or plan.

You only get what you pay for !

There are, fortunately, some benefits to be had from the multiple permutation. Most importantly the pools investor can

**A pools entry
which makes use
of forecast ratings
- figure 30**

manipulate the number of selections and lines submitted, and hence the cost of the bet. Treble Chance entries of this kind are also easy to check. Simply count up the points totals for the best of the permutations in each column. For the entry in figure 29 these are the highest points obtained from four selections in each of the two columns.

Here is another way to make use of multiple permutations.

You may think that certain draw forecasts are more likely to prove correct than others. If so, try to distribute selections, and choose permutations, in such a way as to reflect the differences in your prediction ratings.

Perhaps you have developed a method to rank draw forecasts, or have noticed that score draws seem to be more frequent in certain league divisions than others.

Consider the example in figure 30. A total of 19 selections have been made in *one* column of the coupon. The selections have been divided into three sets. The permutations making up this entry are, from top to bottom, 2 from 5, 3 from 6 and 3 from 8. This gives a total of 11200 lines (10 X 20 X 56).

In each of the three sets, the permuted number divided by the number of selections, and expressed as a percentage, is an indicator of the confidence with which the draw selections are made....

2 from 5 = (2 / 5) X 100 = 40.0%
3 from 6 = (3 / 6) X 100 = 50.0%
3 from 8 = (3 / 8) X 100 = 37.5%

In this coupon entry the distribution of draw

selections and choice of permutations have been based upon the finding that the largest proportion of score draws previously appeared in the division covered by the second set of selections.

Remember that, unless cup games are being played, the matches from the same football leagues and divisions are invariably grouped together on a pools coupon.

The first and third set of selections were chosen because the matches in those divisions have previously delivered the next best levels of drawn results.

Of course this approach makes the assumption that the distribution of draws throughout each division will continue in the future as it has in the past. In addition, for each match selection, there are still important decisions to be made concerning the relative abilities of the opposing teams. Each match must be considered on its merits.

Finally, it must be said that a single full cover permutation which makes use of the top 16 of these 19 draw forecasts (and consists of a similar number of lines) might prove equally successful. The advantages of one approach over the other are difficult to assess.

Block Perms

The pools enthusiast will encounter plans in the form of 'block perms'.

In figure 28 the thirty lines of a pools plan were written out in full, but by permuting columns of Xs, in two or more blocks of selections, a large

A Treble Chance plan using block perms - figure 31

(grid chart of Xs)

BLOCK PERMS

This plan uses block perms to provide 100 lines (10 X 10). Use this as a checking chart for the plan.

The coupon is marked out with 20 draw selections down one column, as figure 32 shows.

62

Match forecasts for the plan described in *figure 31* are arranged in one column of 20 selections - figure 32

number of lines can be represented in a much reduced space.

Figure 31 shows a simple plan consisting of a 10 X 10 block perm.

Assuming that this is a 'named' plan, the entry would consist of 20 score draw selections down a single column of the coupon (see figure 32).

Remember that when coupons are submitted the pools firm must be made aware of the plan being used. Plans are identified by a unique name and number. The name is either selected from those listed on the pools coupon or it is inserted by the punter adjacent to the column of match selections.

Look again at figure 31. There are two blocks of 10 columns. In each block there are 10 rows. Each row represents one match selection. Four of the selections in each column are identified with an 'X'.

The individual treble chance lines are created by pairing off columns from the upper and lower blocks. This pairing process creates 100 different combinations of eight X's. Each line is constructed using 4 X's from the top block and 4 X's from the bottom block.

This method of permuting columns from two or more blocks is something with which the pools punter will quickly become familiar.

A block perm of the size in figure 31 is easily checked.

Write down the points gained for each of the predicted results. This has been done in the figure opposite.

The next step is to check each column of each block and calculate the points obtained. It is of course possible to create a checking template of the kind previously described. However, for explanatory purposes, the complete plan has been displayed again in figure 33 and the points for the 20 match selections inserted against the left-most column of each block.

	TREBLE CHA		
	Place an 'X' -		
1			-
2			-
3			-
4			-
5	X		- 2
6			-
7	X		- 3
8			-
9	X		- 1
10			-
11			-
12			-
13			-
14			-
15			-
16	X		- 2
17			-
18	X		- 3
19			-
20	X		- 1
21			-
22	X		- 1
23	X		- 3
24			-
25			-
26			-
27	X		- 1
28	X		- 3
29	X		- 3
30			-
31			-
32			-
33			-
34	X		- 1
35	X		- 1
36			-
37			-
38	X		- 2
39			-
40			-
41			-
42	X		- 3
43			-
44			-
45			-
46	X		- 1
47			-
48	X		- 1
49			-
50	X		- 3
51	X		- 3
52			-
53	X		- 1
54			-
55			-
56			-
57			-
58			-

Checking the points gained in each column of a block perm - figure 33

Note : this is the plan shown in figure 31, and the selections are those on the coupon in figure 32

	1	2	3	4	5	6	7	8	9	10
2				X			X		X	X
3			X			X		X		X
1		X			X			X	X	
2	X				X	X	X			
3	X	X	X	X						
1			X		X		X	X		
1		X				X	X		X	
3		X		X	X					X
1	X		X						X	X
3	X			X		X		X		
	9	8	8	11	7	9	6	8	5	9

	1	2	3	4	5	6	7	8	9	10
3				X			X		X	X
1			X			X		X		X
1		X			X			X	X	
2	X				X	X	X			
3	X	X	X	X						
1			X		X		X	X		
1		X				X	X		X	
3		X		X	X					X
3	X		X						X	X
1	X			X		X		X		
	9	8	8	10	7	5	7	4	8	10

The points are listed in the same order in which they appear in the coupon (see figure 32).

Where there is an X in the column take note of the number of points gained. Add up the points gained for the 4 selections marked X in a column, and enter the total at the foot of the column.

To find the highest scoring line of 8 selections, add the best points total from the top and bottom blocks. In figure 33 the best column in the upper block produced 11 points. In the lower block two columns gained 10 points. Consequently, two lines on this football coupon have gained 21 points.

You could of course go on to calculate the points gained for all 100 lines. However if you know the maximum points gained this will generally be enough to indicate the kind of prize you can expect.

It is worth noting that from the 20 match selections in figure 32, *eight* were correctly predicted as score draws. This gives a potential 24 points... but in practice only 21 points were obtained.. This is hardly surprising. A full

---

Examples of 'utility' blocks - figure 34

BLOCK 'A'
This is an extract from a block consisting of 60 columns, with 4 draw selections in each column.
If there are 6 draws in the 12 selections, 4 will be correct.

BLOCK 'B'
This is the start of a block consisting of 100 columns, with 4 draw selections in each column.
If any 3 of the 14 selections are correct they will be together in one column.

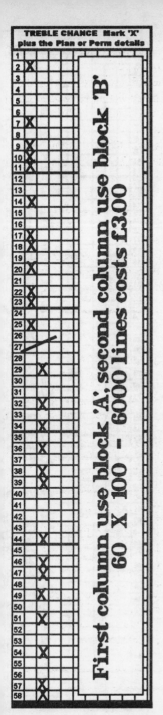

A pools entry
which uses
'utility' blocks
- figure 35

65

cover permutation of 8 from 20, which is the *only* guarantee of a 1st dividend with eight correct selections, would require 125,970 lines !

Finally, you may have noticed that the same pattern of selections has been used in both the upper and lower blocks of this particular plan. This is by no means always the case, as you will discover when reading the next section... 'utility' blocks.

Utility Blocks

Many pools plans consist of block perms of the kind just described, but the pools companies also provide individual blocks of selections which can be used by the pools punter to 'construct' coupon entries.

These 'utility' blocks go by various names. *Brittens Pools* describe them as 'Pick & Mix' blocks, *Littlewoods* as 'Lit-Blocks', *Vernons* as 'Couplems' and *Zetters* as 'Zeep' blocks. Each block is identified by a unique reference number and carries a guarantee.

Consider figure 34. The first block consists of 12 selections and guarantees that if there are 6 score draws there will be 4 together in one column. Utility block 'A' uses 60 columns. The second block gives a guarantee for 14 selections. If there are 3 score draws in block 'B' they will occur together in at least one of the columns. There are 100 columns in block 'B'.

Combining these two blocks in one pools entry requires a total of 26 selections. Select 12 matches in one column of the

A Pools Entry using Permutations, Consecutive Selections and a 'Lit-Block' - figure 36

66

coupon and 14 in the next. Don't forget that the same match cannot appear in more than one column. Such an error would invalidate the entry.

Instructions are included on the coupon as shown in figure 35

Note that the total number of treble chance lines submitted is 6000 (60 X 100).

The total cost of the bet is of course determined by the cost per line. In this example the cost happens to be low. It is 20 lines for one penny This requires a payment of £3.00 for the pools entry.

An alternative entry might use either of these two blocks *twice*. If block 'B' were chosen, a total of 28 selections (14 + 14) would be required, giving 10,000 lines (100 X 100).

Utility blocks take many shapes and sizes and often more than two blocks form an entry. For example three blocks might be used. Two blocks could each contribute 3 X's, and one block 2 X's, to each treble chance line. With, let us say, 20 columns in each of two blocks, and 30 in the third, such an entry gives 12,000 lines (20 X 20 X 30). It need hardly be said that the checking process would be extremely laborious.

Summary

It is possible to combine all manner of selections, permutations and blocks.

In figures 36 and 38 composite entries have been constructed to help demonstrate just how this can be done.

Consider figure 36. The entry has three columns. The first is labelled 'A'. It is a straight permutation of 2 from 5 selections.

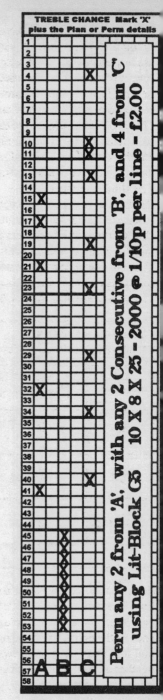

It contributes 2 X's and generates 10 lines.

Column 'B' has 9 match selections with instructions to use any two *consecutive* selections. These 9 selections consist of *eight pairs* of consecutive matches.

In this instance the column of X's represents both consecutive match numbers and consecutive selections.

This need not always be the case, as was explained on page 55. Identifying each selection by its match number, the consecutive selections are 45,46 / 46,47 / 47,48 / etc. The total number of consecutive *pairs* is always one less than the number of selections. Eight pairs of X's in this case.

The third column in figure 36 refers to a utility block. The 'Lit-Block' represented in column 'C' contributes 4 X's to each treble chance line. This requires 9 match selections and the block consists of 25 columns.

The written instructions describe the structure of the bet and show the number of lines, the cost per line and total stake.

The constituent parts of the pools entry are shown in figure 37.

The pools entry in *figure 36* summarised - figure 37

Coupon Column	treble chance X's	match selections	lines or columns
'A'	2	5	10
'B'	2	9	8
'C'	4	9	25
Totals	8	23	2000

Each column contributes a specified number of X's to each treble chance line. There must be eight X's in a line. There can be a variable number of *match selections* in each column, but each match selection can appear only once in the entry. Each coupon column contributes a number of lines to the multiple entry. It is the *product* of these lines which determines the total number of 'betting' lines submitted.

A Pools Entry using a 'Brit-Block', Non-Consecutive Selections and Paired Selections - figure 38

Figure 38 presents another multiple entry. Again there are three columns.

Column 'A' is a 'Brit-Block'. This is a utility block which contributes 4 X's to the treble chance line. It uses 50 block columns and requires 10 match selections.

In coupon column 'B' the match selections are *non-consecutive* pairs. Permuting any 2 from 9 selections gives 28 lines. Referring to the coupon numbers, non-consecutive pairs of selections are 45,47 / 45,48 / 45,49 / etc.

Column 'C' consists of 5 pairs of selections. Any one of these pairs provides the 2 X's required to complete each treble chance line. The entire entry is summarised in figure 39. There are 7000 lines, but at 1/20 of a penny per line the cost is kept down.

It is advisable to stake the minimum allowable per line. This amount will be printed on the pools coupon. Any increase in the total stake you are prepared to risk is best invested in the purchase of extra lines.

 It is easy to calculate the total number of lines in a non-consecutive permutation.
Suppose the non-consecutive permutation is 'perm x from y'. Calculate, or read from a table, the number of lines which would be generated by permuting 'x from y-x+1'.
Thus, the number of non-consecutive lines of 2 from 9 is ....

$$2 \text{ from } (9-2+1) = 2 \text{ from } 8 = 28$$

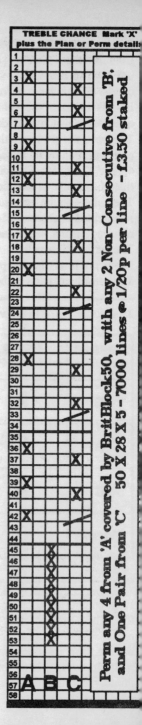

TREBLE CHANCE Mark 'X' plus the Plan or Perm details

Perm any 4 from 'A' covered by BritBlock50, with any 2 Non-Consecutive from 'B', and One Pair from 'C' 50 X 28 X 5 - 7000 lines @ 1/20p per line - £3.50 staked

A B C

You will see in figure 38 that grouped selections need not always appear in separate columns. A single column of selections can be divided using a series of horizontal lines. But you must ensure that the accompanying written instructions make the structure of the bet absolutely clear.

The pools entry in *figure 38* summarised - figure 39

Coupon Column	treble chance X's	match selections	lines or columns
'A'	4	10	50
'B'	2	9	28
'C'	2	10	5
Totals	8	29	7000

It is also important that any 'named' entry you use is known to the pools company with which it is submitted. The Pools Promoters Association keep a register of pools plans and blocks which are acceptable.

Forth Dimension
28 Macbeth Road
Dunfermline.
KY11 4EG

Many correspondents have expressed an interest in pools plans and perms. 'Forth Dimension' has close contacts with a number of acknowledged experts in the field who have expressed a willingness to provide advice and examples. If you require help, drop us a line. Please enclose two 1st class postage stamps and your correspondence will be forwarded.

Probabilities and Betting Odds

It is not at all unusual to hear people speak of the 'likelihood' of rain, or the 'chance' of their favourite team winning an important game. These statements tend to be vague and subjective.

Of course it is *possible* to make a subjective judgement concerning the comaparative skills of football teams. In doing so the evaluation of the outcome becomes a measure of an individual's beliefs concerning the relative abilities of opposing teams. This approach might be described as an 'educated guess'. It relies little upon factual evidence, but heavily upon intuition. Surprisingly enough this is *exactly* the way the majority of punters complete pools and fixed-odds coupons. It is not recommended.

The accepted way to to lend some authority to pronouncements about the outcome of future events, and to quantify the uncertainties involved, is to assign them *probability* values (or, as will be discussed shortly, to specify *odds*).

PROBABILITIES

The probability of a given event occurring is said to lie between the extremes **0** and **1**. If it is thought that something *cannot possibly happen* then the probability is **zero**. If it is *completely certain* to take place, the probability is **one**. You will find that probabilities are represented as fractions (eg **3/4**), as decimals (**0.75**), or percentages (**75%**).

The concept of probabilities was first applied to those games of chance where all possible outcomes are equally likely. In such cases it is not difficult to calculate values in advance, *before* the event takes place. For example the probability of tossing a 'head' with a balanced coin is clearly **1/2,** or of rolling a '2' with a die **1/6**.

The difficulty with this basic approach is that it can be applied only in a limited number of situations. In day to day life the possibilities that arise cannot always be established so easily. This is the case, for example, if an attempt is made to estimate the chance of snow falling on Christmas day. The answer to such a problem rests with past experience. It is necessary to study meteorological records over a period of several years. The probability of this event can then be expressed as the number of times there was snow on Christmas day, out of the total number of Christmas days researched.

In assessing probabilities in this way the assumption is made that events will occur in the same proportions in the future as they have in the past.

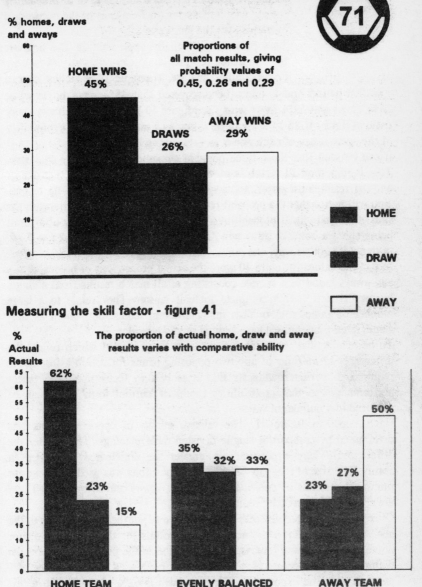

Proportions of homes, draws and aways - figure 40

71

% homes, draws
and aways

Proportions of
all match results, giving
probability values of
0.45, 0.26 and 0.29

HOME WINS
45%

DRAWS
26%

AWAY WINS
29%

HOME

DRAW

AWAY

Measuring the skill factor - figure 41

%
Actual
Results

The proportion of actual home, draw and away
results varies with comparative ability

62%

23%

15%

35%

32%   33%

23%

27%

50%

HOME TEAM
SUPERIOR

EVENLY BALANCED
TEAMS

AWAY TEAM
SUPERIOR

The best rated 5% of potential home wins, draws and away wins were
analysed. Categories are determined by relative league positions.

Insurance policies are based on this kind of probability theory, which measures the frequency of the occurrence of events over the long-term.

This principle is equally applicable in the analysis football match results.

For example, analyse a sample of matches over a specified period and it might be discovered that **45%** were home wins, **26%** draws and **29%** away wins (see figure 40). **The home, draw, away ratio of 0.45 : 0.26 : 0.29 can be taken as a measure of the probability of the occurrence of each result in future matches.**

It can be seen that these three possible outcomes are mutually exclusive. That is, if a football match is played to a finish, it is certain that one or another result must occur. Consequently the probabilities add up to one. You will notice that the probability of either of two results occurring is the sum of the individual probabilities. For instance the probability of a result being either a home or away win *(ie not a draw)* is **0.45 + 0.29 = 0.74,** or to put it another way, one minus the probability of a draw.

In fact the values in figure 40 were the actual proportions of homes, draws and aways found in a sample consisting of all match results from a single league division over a complete football season. They relate to a large number of games and involve many different teams, but, taken as they stand, these probabilities have limited predictive value.

To be of practical use, probabilities must be generated which reflect the differences in *abilities* of any two opposing teams for which a forecast is required. Experience suggests that it is best to focus upon the recent performances so that probabilities represent 'current form'. This can be achieved in a number of ways.

Have a look at figure 41. The relative quality of opposing teams was determined by comparing league division table placings. The greater the difference in league position the greater the anticipated difference in ability. The size of the 'gap' between team positions was used to categorise imminent matches as *potential* home wins, draws and away wins. These are effectively the match predictions.

Over a period of several weeks it was decided to put these predictions to the test. The figure shows the actual match results for the *top-rated 5%* of home, draw and away forecasts. The variation in the proportions of results within each prediction category is quite pronounced. You will see, for example, that the expectation of a home win is 62% when the top teams play at home against lowly opposition. Compare this with the 45% value encountered above.

It can now be said that, for the top-rated 5% of home forecasts, the probabilities for the outcome of a match are ...

home win=62%   draw=23%   away win=15%

Similarly, figure 41 shows probabilities for results
where the teams are evenly matched or the away team
is considered superior.

In fact, if the sample size is sufficiently large, it is possible to compute the
probability of a home win, draw or away win for the full range of
differences in league table placings. Such an exercise is likely to produce a
distribution of values very similar to that shown in figure 10, on page 19.

In the above example predictions were based upon league position.
However, other prediction criteria, such as league points or goals scored,
could prove more effective. Results prediction is of course the subject of
the first section of *Football Fortunes*, and several prediction rating systems
have been considered in some detail.

In practice there are many alternative approaches to the calculation of
probabilities, but whatever the method, the aim is to quantify, as
realistically as is practicable, the uncertainties associated with results
forecasting.

In each case the computed probabilities are determined by the 'relative
frequencies' of past results and will form the basis of match predictions. In
addition, given these empirical probabilities, it is a simple matter to
calculate betting odds. This is explained below.

PROBABILITIES TO ODDS

It has been pointed out that if all possible outcomes are known in a specific
set of circumstances then the sum of the probabilities of each outcome must
equal **1**. So, given the probability of **1/6** *(or 0.1666)* that a '2' be thrown
with a die, it follows that the chance of throwing any number *other* than '2'
is **1 minus 1/6 = 5/6** *(or 0.8333)*.

It can be seen that the ratio of *throwing* to *not throwing* a '2' is **1/6** to **5/6**.
By discarding the common denominator of six, the ratio of success to
failure may be re-stated as **1 to 5**. *These are the mathematical odds.*

Mathematical odds may be defined as the ratio of the probability that an
event *will* occur to the probability that it *will not* occur. It is customary to
express odds in terms of two positive integers without the common factor.

In the preceding case the odds could be written as **1-5** or **1/5**. However it is
the latter representation of odds which is most often encountered. So odds
will be shown in this book as **1/5**, **11/10**, **3/1**, etc. Consequently, to avoid
confusion with odds, probabilities are best depicted, not as a fraction, but as

74

a decimal or percentage.

It should be clearly understood that in the world of football gambling the approach to odds is somewhat different to that taken by the mathematician, and great care must be taken to avoid errors or confusion. There are two frequent causes of mis-understanding.

First of all, if *betting odds* equal the *true* mathematical odds *(and hence reflect true probability)* they are technically said to be 'fair' odds. An unfortunate term, for when it comes to bets placed with a bookmaker, the bookie's odds are never fair !

The bookie manipulates odds in his own favour to achieve a pre-determined *profit margin* or over-round. This is not, of course, to question the integrity of the bookmakers, it simply reflects the need to make a business profit ! The precise workings and effects of the bookies' profit margin will be considered in due course, but for now it is useful, for explanatory purposes, to start from the premise that betting odds are indeed fair odds.

The second cause of confusion concerns the *presentation* of betting odds. Take the situation where the probability of a draw has been estimated as **0.25**. It follows that the sum of the probabilities of other results occurring is **1 - 0.25 = 0.75**. However the bookmaker would quote the odds *against* a draw as **0.75** to **0.25**, that is **3/1**. This is not at first sight what one might intuitively expect, in so far as odds expressed in this way represent the ratio of the non-occurrence of a draw to the occurrence of a draw, seemingly a reversal of the success to failure ratio previously encountered. However the terms success and failure are used rather loosely. What is favourable to one individual may be unfavourable to another.... and this is never more apparent than in the relationship between the bookmaker and his client.

The important lesson is that the bookie's 'offer' is shown to the left and the punter's 'stake' to the right. To put this another way, the value on the right is the amount risked by the punter to win that on the left.

Odds are often described by the bookmaker as *prices*.... and these may be *even money, odds against* or *odds on*.

If bets are *'even money'* the potential payout by the bookie equals the amount risked by the gambler. If £1 were staked, the winnings for a successful bet would be £1. On fixed-odds football coupons you will find even money odds represented as **Evens, Evn** or **1/1**.

All prices, other than even money, can be expressed as *'odds against'*. For example, consider odds of **3/1** *against* a draw. A successful bet would *win* £3 for every £1 wagered. Other examples are **9/2, 6/4, 11/10, 10/11, 4/5** and **1/3** against.

Bets may be described as *'odds on'*. In this case, if you win, the bookmaker

Bookies odds, returns and probabilities - figure 42

Odds (i)		Odds ? / 1 (ii)	Return per unit (iii)	Probability decimal & % (iv) (v)	
1/8		0.125/1	1.125	0.8888	88.88
2/15		0.133/1	1.133	0.8824	88.24
1/7		0.143/1	1.143	0.8725	87.25
2/13		0.154/1	1.154	0.8666	86.66
1/6		0.167/1	1.167	0.8571	85.71
2/11		0.182/1	1.182	0.8462	84.62
1/5		0.200/1	1.200	0.8333	83.33
2/9		0.222/1	1.222	0.8182	81.82
1/4		0.250/1	1.250	0.8000	80.00
2/7		0.286/1	1.286	0.7778	77.78
3/10		0.300/1	1.300	0.7692	76.92
1/3		0.333/1	1.333	0.7500	75.00
4/11		0.363/1	1.363	0.7333	73.33
2/5	h	0.400/1	1.400	0.7143	71.43
4/9	h	0.444/1	1.444	0.6923	69.23
1/2	h	0.500/1	1.500	0.6667	66.67
8/15	h	0.533/1	1.533	0.6522	65.22
4/7	h	0.571/1	1.571	0.6364	63.64
8/13	h	0.615/1	1.615	0.6190	61.90
4/6	h	0.667/1	1.667	0.6000	60.00
8/11	h	0.727/1	1.727	0.5789	57.89
4/5	h	0.800/1	1.800	0.5555	55.55
5/6	h	0.833/1	1.833	0.5455	54.55
10/11	h	0.909/1	1.909	0.5238	52.38
1/1	h	1.000/1	2.000	0.5000	50.00
11/10	h	1.100/1	2.100	0.4762	47.62
6/5	h	1.200/1	2.200	0.4545	45.45
5/4	h a	1.250/1	2.250	0.4444	44.44
11/8	h a	1.375/1	2.375	0.4211	42.11
6/4	h a	1.500/1	2.500	0.4000	40.00
8/5	h a	1.600/1	2.600	0.3846	38.46
13/8	h a	1.625/1	2.625	0.3810	38.10
7/4	h a	1.750/1	2.750	0.3636	36.36
9/5	h a	1.800/1	2.800	0.3571	35.71
15/8	D a	1.875/1	2.875	0.3478	34.78
2/1	D a	2.000/1	3.000	0.3334	33.34
11/5	D a	2.200/1	3.200	0.3125	31.25
9/4	D a	2.250/1	3.250	0.3077	30.77
12/5	D	2.400/1	3.400	0.2941	29.41
5/2	D	2.500/1	3.500	0.2857	28.57
13/5	D	2.600/1	3.600	0.2778	27.78
11/4	a	2.750/1	3.750	0.2667	26.67
14/5	a	2.800/1	3.800	0.2632	26.32
3/1	a	3.000/1	4.000	0.2500	25.00
10/3	a	3.333/1	4.333	0.2308	23.08
7/2	a	3.500/1	4.500	0.2222	22.22
18/5	a	3.600/1	4.600	0.2174	21.74
4/1	a	4.000/1	5.000	0.2000	20.00
9/2	a	4.500/1	5.500	0.1818	18.18
5/1	a	5.000/1	6.000	0.1667	16.67
11/2	a	5.500/1	6.500	0.1538	15.38
6/1		6.000/1	7.000	0.1429	14.29
13/2		6.500/1	7.500	0.1334	13.34
7/1		7.000/1	8.000	0.1250	12.50
15/2		7.500/1	8.500	0.1176	11.76
8/1		8.000/1	9.000	0.1111	11.11
17/2		8.500/1	9.500	0.1053	10.53
9/1		9.000/1	10.00	0.1000	10.00
10/1		10.00/1	11.00	0.0909	9.09
12/1		12.00/1	13.00	0.0769	7.69

LOWEST ODDS AND RETURN. MOST PROBABLE.

MOST HOMES IN THIS REGION

MOST DRAWS IN THIS REGION

MOST AWAYS IN THIS REGION

BEST ODDS AND RETURN. LEAST PROBABLE.

pays out less than the amount staked.

Odds on values can sometimes lead to confusion. You have just seen that certain bets may be **10/11** against, **4/5** against, etc. In such cases the left-hand part of the odds figure is *less* than the right-hand part. This means that, for example, with a successful bet at **1/2 against**, you would win £1 for every £2 wagered. The cause of mis-understanding is that, frequently in horse-racing, and occasionally in football betting, you will see such odds offered as '*2/1 on*', stated as *"two to one on"*. It should be realised that this is just the same as the price of 1/2 against. A fixed-odds football coupon lists prices *only* in the 'odds against' format.

The range of numerical values used to denote betting odds is restricted. This is a direct consequence of long-standing tradition, and an unwillingness of the bookie to change with the times. In column (i), of figure 42, the values most regularly found on coupons have been listed.

You will notice that there are some untidy fractions. The logic of their use owes much to the nature of the pre-decimalisation currency of the UK. The fact that there were ten florins, eight half-crowns or four crowns to a pound accounts for the frequent use of 10's, 8's and 4's in odds such as 11/10, 11/8, 15/8, 7/4, etc. The introduction of decimal currency made a few bets easier to settle, but in general the computations, based on prices determined by the pre-1971 currency, have become more difficulty and tedious.

There is another problem. Until the newcomer to fixed-odds betting becomes acquainted with the use of odds, it is not always immediately clear whether one price represents better or poorer value than another. Are odds of 6/4 or 8/5 to be preferred when placing a bet ?

To help resolve this difficulty the odds in figure 42 have been sorted, from top to bottom, in ascending order. That is, the prices are listed from *short* odds (*1/8*), to *long* odds (*12/1*). Furthermore, the fractional values have been evaluated and expressed in column (ii) as a common ratio. Quite simply the odd's numerator has been divided by the denominator. It can now be seen that odds of **6/4** are *less generous* than those of **8/5**, being equivalent, respectively, to odds of **1.5/1** and **1.6/1**.

Many of these problems could be avoided if bookmakers in the UK were to adopt the 'decimal' representation used extensively throughout the rest of Europe. The football coupon would then show the total return for a one unit bet. This is the value in column (iii) of figure 42. Such a step would greatly simplify the calculation of winnings.

Of prime importance to the gambler is the monetary return on his stake. Consider a price of **6/4**. You will now know that the second figure represents the number of units staked by the punter to win the first.

Therefore a bet of £4 at this price would, if successful, win £6.... *but in addition the gambler's stake of £4 is refunded, giving a total return of £10.*

Occasionally the novice expresses surprise that both winnings *and* stake are returned. This is because you are effectively wagering your money *against* that of the bookmaker. The odds represent the *ratio* of the bookmaker's stake to that of the punter.

To understand this a little better, consider two individuals who are betting against each other on the toss of a coin. Their respective bets might be placed in a common kitty. The eventual winner will take the 'pot', which holds the wager of *both* participants. In fixed-odds betting the bookmaker retains custody of the pot, it is hoped temporarily, until the result of the bet has been decided.

One last comment about calculating returns. In the above example the punter risked the loss of £4 to gain £6. Most bets are not so simple, and many require the use of a calculator.

For example, place 50p on a draw at odds of 9/4 ....

Winnings	=	(9 X 50p) / 4	=	112.5p
Return	=	112.5 + 50p	=	162.5p

You could use the information in figure 42 to help make this calculation, where column (iii) shows the total return on a one unit bet. For example, for a win on a single bet of 50p, priced at 9/4, you receive ...

3.25 X 50p = 162.5p

The calculation of returns, including the effect of betting tax, is considered in depth under the heading 'Fixed-Odds Betting'.

BOOKIE'S PROFIT MARGIN

Betting odds are compiled in such a way as to restrict the punter's winnings and thereby increase the bookmaker's profits.

It has been mentioned that when betting odds equal the true odds that an event will occur they are said to be 'fair' odds. So, on the throw of a die, if someone offered to bet £18 against your £4 that a '2' would be the next throw, would the odds be fair ? The answer quite simply is *"no"*.

The probability that a '2' will *not* be thrown is ... **1 minus 1/6 = 5/6**.

This gives true odds of 5 to 1 **against** successfully throwing a '2'.

The bet would have been fair only if the offer had been £20 against £4 that the next throw will be '2'. The ratio of 20:4 being 5:1.

The £18 to £4 bet *favours* the individual staking the £18 !

It is by this means that the bookmaker can be assured of a comfortable living. In the *long-term* the bookie would be more than willing to risk £18 against the punter's £4 (on the throw of a '2', or any other single number in a game of dice) and would be *guaranteed* a profit.

Unless the punter can find an 'edge' of his own, he will *always* lose in the long run because the odds are in favour of the bookmaker. In the preceding example the bookmaker was more than happy to offer a price of 9/2 **against** the throw of any number at dice, when the true odds were 5/1. The massaging of odds, which determines the bookie's **profit margin**, might be said to give a new slant to the expression *fixed*-odds betting !

The bookie's profit has just been described in terms of *reduced odds*. It can equally well be seen as an *increase in probabilities*. The bookmaker artificially boosts the probability, and thereby depresses the odds.

Examine figure 42 and compare the values in columns (i) and (v). You will see that as the odds shorten the probabilites increase. So the direct consequence of a bookmaker offering less than fair odds is that the numerical value of the probability is enhanced.

To make this clear try converting odds to probabilities. For example, consider odds of 5/4 offered for a home win. To calculate the probability divide the integer on the right of the odds by the sum of the component integers ....

$$4 / (4 + 5) = 4/9 = 0.4444$$

You can confirm this from figure 42.

Now, for any match on a fixed-odds football coupon, use this same formula, or refer to the table, to obtain the individual probabilities for a home win, draw and away win. You will invariably find that their sum is greater than 100%. Suppose the odds for a match are ....

Home 5/4   Draw 9/4   Away 7/4

The percentage values add up as follows ....

$$44.45\% + 30.77\% + 36.36\% = 111.35\%$$

The *sum* of the probabilities of all of the outcomes of *any* match on a fixed-odds coupon will *exceed* 100%; but of course, in practice, there can be no greater than 100% certainty of any event taking place. However, this excess does provide a useful measure of a bookie's profit margin or over-round.

In the preceding example the profit margin was a typical **11.35%**. Generally, in football betting, where the result is to be forecast simply as a home, draw or away, the value lies between **10%** and **14%**, although you will discover that the bookie often takes a little more profit out of home win bets, than draws or aways.

Scores, probabilities and profit margin - figure 43

Bookie's Profit Margin on Correct Scores

HOME (result odds = 5/4   probability = 44.45%)

score	1-0	2-0	2-1	3-0	3-1	3-2	4-0, etc
odds	7/1	9/1	7/1	20/1	16/1	25/1	50/1, etc
prob%	12.50	10.00	12.50	4.75	5.88	3.85	6.39

Home Scores Total Probability = **55.88%**

DRAW (result odds = 9/4   probability = 30.77%)

score	0-0	1-1	2-2	3-3, etc
odds	8/1	11/2	14/1	50/1, etc
prob%	11.11	15.38	6.66	1.96

Draw Scores Total Probability = **35.11%**

AWAY (result odds = 7/4   probability = 36.36%)

score	1-0	2-0	2-1	3-0	3-1	3-2	4-0, etc
odds	7/1	12/1	10/1	28/1	25/1	25/1	80/1, etc
prob%	12.50	7.69	9.09	3.57	3.85	3.85	3.69

Away Scores Total Probability = **44.24%**

Total Scores Probability = **135.11%**

In *correct scores* betting the over-round may be as much as **40%**, and, you will recall, the larger this value, the less the relationship to true odds !

Figure 43 shows the margin of profit the bookie demands from correct scores bets. The precise odds for each *score* will of course vary from match to match, so the values in the tables are the odds for scores, where home win, draw and away win are priced, respectively, as **5/4**, **9/4** and **7/4** (*ie the preceding example is continued*).

The odds of **5/4** for a home win, which already include an over-round, convert to a probability of **44.45%**. Add up the percentages for *each possible home win score* and the bookie's probability increases to **55.88%**. There are smaller, but significant increases, in the profit margins for draw and away win scores. The outcome is an over-round of **35.23%** for the complete set of correct score prices.

You must certainly have confidence in your forecasting ability before taking on the bookie with a correct score wager.... but if you think you can do the business there are some correct score coupon entries on page 115.

PRICING MATCHES

It was mentioned that a limited range of values is used by the bookie to represent betting odds. It was also explained that, because of the bookmaker's over-round, the sum of the 'probabilities' for home, draw and away results is in the region of **112%** (**+/- 2%**). The consequence is that this restricts the number of different sets of three values of odds which are available to price a complete match.

In figure 44 most of the odds found on football coupons have been listed. Look at the second column, headed bookie's **'HOME ODDS'**. These are the over-rounded bookmaker's odds for a home victory.

The top row shows the bookie's **'DRAW ODDS'**. Odds for draws cover a small range, with regularly quoted prices being 11/5, 9/4 and 12/5.

Where rows and columns intersect are the bookie's **'AWAY ODDS'**. These complete the set of three odds values necessary to price each match.

Find a match on a fixed-odds coupon with *home odds* of 4/6 and *draw odds* of 12/5, and it is quite possible that the *away win* will be priced at 7/2.... as the table shows.

The precise odds depend upon the bookie's profit margin, which, for the most part, lies between **10%** and **12%**. However, if you carefully look through a fixed-odds coupon, you will find that certain draw odds are occasionally associated with a higher than average over-round for the complete match (*ie between 12% and 13%*). In the table opposite this

COMBINATIONS OF BETTING ODDS

		likely draw		DRAW ODDS			*unlikely draw*		
True Home %	Bookie's HOME ODDS	15/8	2/1	11/5	9/4	12/5	5/2	13/5	11/4
65.0	2/5	17/1	13/1	10/1	10/1	8/1	7/1	7/1	13/2
62.5	4/9	13/1	10/1	8/1	15/2	6/1	13/2	6/1	11/2
60.0	1/2	9/1	15/2	13/2	6/1	11/2	5/1	5/1	9/2
59.0	8/15	8/1	13/2	11/2	11/2	5/1	9/2	9/2	4/1
57.5	4/7	7/1	6/1	5/1	5/1	9/2	4/1	4/1	4/1
56.0	8/13	6/1	5/1	9/2	9/2	4/1	7/2	7/2	10/3
54.0	4/6	5/1	9/2	4/1	4/1	7/2	10/3	3/1	3/1
52.0	8/11	9/2	4/1	7/2	10/3	12/5	3/1	14/5	11/4
50.0	4/5	4/1	18/5	3/1	3/1	11/4	13/5	13/5	12/5
49.0	5/6	18/5	7/2	14/5	11/4	13/5	12/5	12/5	9/4
47.0	10/11	10/3	3/1	13/5	5/2	12/5	11/5	11/5	11/5
45.0	1/1	14/5	5/2	9/4	9/4	11/5	2/1	2/1	15/8
43.0	11/10	12/5	9/4	11/5	2/1	15/8	7/4	7/4	7/4
41.0	6/5	9/4	11/5	15/8	9/5	7/4	13/8	13/8	8/5
40.0	5/4	11/5	2/1	9/5	7/4	13/8	6/4	8/5	6/4
38.0	11/8	15/8	7/4	13/8	8/5	6/4	11/8	11/8	11/8
36.0	6/4	7/4	8/5	6/4	6/4	11/8	11/8	5/4	5/4
34.5	8/5	13/8	6/4	11/8	11/8	11/8	5/4	6/5	6/5
34.0	13/8	8/5	6/4	11/8	11/8	5/4	6/5	6/5	6/5
33.0	7/4	6/4	11/8	5/4	5/4	6/5	11/10	11/10	11/10
32.0	9/5	6/4	11/8	5/4	6/5	6/5	11/10	11/10	11/10
31.5	15/8	11/8	11/8	6/5	6/5	11/10	11/10	11/10	1/1
30.0	2/1	11/8	5/4	6/5	11/10	11/10	1/1	1/1	1/1
28.0	11/5	6/5	6/5	11/10	1/1	1/1	10/11	10/11	10/11
27.5	9/4	6/5	11/10	1/1	1/1	1/1	10/11	10/11	5/6
26.5	12/5	11/10	11/10	1/1	1/1	10/11	5/6	5/6	4/5
25.5	5/2	11/10	1/1	1/1	10/11	10/11	5/6	5/6	4/5
25.0	13/5	11/10	1/1	10/11	10/11	5/6	4/5	4/5	4/5
24.0	11/4	1/1	1/1	10/11	5/6	4/5	4/5	4/5	8/11
23.5	14/5	1/1	10/11	10/11	5/6	4/5	8/11	8/11	8/11
22.5	3/1	10/11	10/11	5/6	4/5	8/11	8/11	8/11	4/6
20.5	10/3	10/11	5/6	4/5	8/11	8/11	4/6	4/6	8/13
20.0	7/2	5/6	4/5	8/11	8/11	4/6	8/13	8/13	8/13

AWAY ODDS

occurs in several sets of prices which include draw odds of 5/2. This enhanced over-round seems to apply largely to matches in the lower Scottish Divisions.

The table in figure 44 can also be used to price matches. It is only a guide, but comes close to the values found on most fixed-odds coupon.

To price a game make use of the league table data commonly available in newspapers and on television. Each team must have played a minimum of 12 matches in the current season. If not, you will have to include the previous season's data.

Take an example where the current number of wins, draws and losses, in a league table, for *two opposing teams* is as follows ...

```
team 1                        team 2
Home results                  Away results
wins    draws   losses        wins    draws   losses
12(hW)  6(hD)   3(hL)         4(aW)   6(aD)   11(aL)
```

This is the data which will be used to calculate the value **'True Home %'** in the table in figure 44. In the football match for which odds are to be calculated, *team 1* is playing at home and *team 2* away. The number of **home wins** of the home team is *added* to the **away losses** of the away team. This value is then *multiplied* by **100** and *divided* by the **total number** of games played by *both* teams. The formula is simply ....

```
( ( home wins + away losses ) X 100 ) / ( total games )
```

Note that 'total games', in this calculation, refers to the sum of the home games played by the home team and of the away games played by the away team. So using the data above, total games played equals ....

```
12(hW)+6(hD)+3(hL)+4(aW)+6(aD)+11(aL) = 42
```

The 'True Home %' value is therefore ....

```
( 23(hW+aL) X 100 ) / 42  = 54.7
```

The next step is to locate the 'True Home %' listed in the first column of the table, which is *closest* to the value just calculated. In this example **54.0** is nearest to **54.7**. Now read the value of bookie's 'HOME ODDS' from the adjacent column. The home odds for this match are therefore **4/6**. Remember these odds values include the bookie's over-round.

The next step is to examine the draw prices. The higher priced odds, for example **13/5** and **11/4**, are reckoned to represent those matches *less likely* to end in a draw, while odds such as **15/8** or **2/1** are thought *more likely* to be drawn games. However, the variation across the range of odds for draws is minimal when compared to homes and aways. This reflects the increased difficulty in forecasting draws. To select the odds for a draw you must make an arbitrary judgement. In this case it might be thought that the chances of a draw are best represented by odds of **12/5**.

The last stage is to find the point on the table where the home row and draw column intersect. In the continuing example this is at the price of **7/2**. These are the away odds for this match.

The match has now been priced as.....

     home 4/6   draw 12/5   away 7/2

It was suggested that the 'raw data' used to compile these odds should be taken directly from league tables. You could equally well use a *recent sequence* of matches. For example, why not try the last 6 home games of the home team and the last 6 away games of the away team. This would better reflect the *current form* of the opposing teams.

Should it happen that, in calculating the 'True Home %', the computed value exceeds 65.0%, or is less than 20.0%, simply take the respective home odds of 2/5 and 7/2. (*After all, the bookmaker does not tolerate extreme prices, regardless of how slim the prospects of payout !*).

This method provides an approximation to the bookmaker's prices. On page 125 the approach has been developed, and a computer algorithm which compiles betting odds, has been described in some detail.

Finally, the graphics in figure 45 (*below and overleaf*) depict the range and proportions of odds assigned to home wins, draws and away wins on a typical fixed-odds coupon.

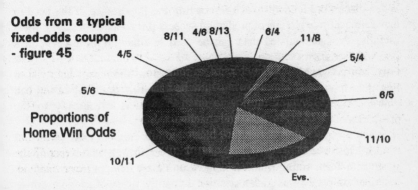

Odds from a typical fixed-odds coupon - figure 45

Proportions of Home Win Odds

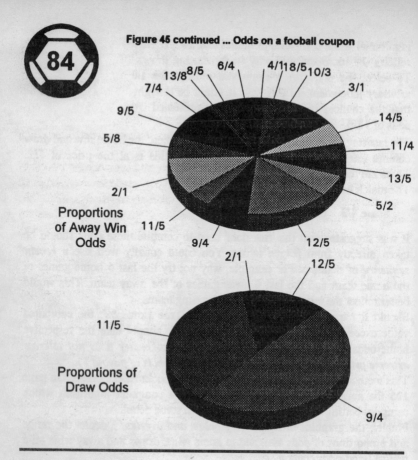

Figure 45 continued ... Odds on a fooball coupon

84

Figure labels (Proportions of Away Win Odds): 13/8 8/5 6/4 4/1 18/5 10/3, 7/4, 9/5, 5/8, 2/1, 11/5, 9/4, 2/1, 12/5, 5/2, 13/5, 11/4, 14/5, 3/1

Proportions of Away Win Odds

Figure labels (Proportions of Draw Odds): 2/1, 12/5, 11/5, 9/4

Proportions of Draw Odds

FORECASTING SUCCESS RATES AND ODDS

When discussing football match forecasting the importance of the need to maintain accurate records of prediction success rates was emphasised. Most usefully, the accumulated data can be used to find the 'best bets' on a fixed-odds coupon.

Carry out an analysis of the kind described below and it will help you to find the match forecasts which, *if applied over the long-term*, can *guarantee* a profit. This particular example refers specifically to the prediction of home wins.

In many approches to forecasting a 'points difference' is used to predict results. This value is calculated for each and every match by subtracting the away team 'form' rating from the home team rating. The 'rateform' method, described on page 12, is such a system.

If records of forecasting success rates are analysed over a sufficiently long period a mathematical relationship can be established between forecasting success rates and points difference values.

Have a glance at the table in figure 46. You will see, for example, that of the home forecasts analysed which had a points difference of +300, 51.44% resulted in home wins. Similarly a points difference of -300 gave 28.06% home wins.

To make practical use of such data it is necessary to consider the effects of betting tax. To this end an 'adjustment' has been made to the calculated success rate. Let the tax rate be, for the sake of simplicity, 10%. The success rates have been reduced by this amount to give tax adjusted values as shown in column (iii) of figure 46. Calculate a tax *adjusted success rate* (aSR) for a series of points difference (PD) values.

You can now begin to identify the 'best bets' on a fixed-odds coupon.

First of all, for each value of home win odds given on the fixed-odds coupon, calculate the *'probability'* of a home win.... or read the probability from the table in figure 42 *(eg the probability for odds of 6/4 = 40.00%)*. Bookie's odds, with their respective probabilities, have been listed in columns (ii) and (iii) of figure 47. Next, using the chosen prediction method, calculate the points difference for each pair of competing teams, and insert the relevant adjusted success rate (see columns (iv) and (v) in figure 47).

The final step is to compare the bookie's probability (P), column (iii), with the adjusted success rate, column (v). For each match in which the adjusted success rate *exceeds* the bookie's probability the punter has been given *better* than 'fair' odds. *If wagers, using these identified matches, are submitted over a sufficiently long period, you must make a profit.*

Use the selected matches to place singles, doubles, trebles or other small accumulators. Provided success rates have been accurately assessed, all wager should favour the gambler.

To develop this system a little further a graph can be prepared (figure 48) which plots points difference against success rate. A simple formula can then be devised which converts points difference directly to adjusted success rate, whatever the value of the points difference happens to be.

In this example, for the sake of simplicity, it has been assumed that the relationship is adequately represented by a straight line. Furthermore the equation has been based only upon the values of points difference of +300 and -300, where the adjusted success rates were, respectively, 46.30% and 25.26%. It was for these values that most data had been collected.

Calculating the tax adjusted forecasting success rate - figure 46

```
Points Difference and
Forecasting Success Rate

   points          forecast        success rate
 difference        success         adjusted
home rating       rate(%)          for tax(%)
  (i) PD           (ii) SR         (iii) aSR


  +1500            97.67              87.91
  +1200            88.66              79.80
  + 900            73.93              66.54
  + 600            64.22              57.80
  + 300            51.44              46.30
   zero            39.50              35.55
  - 300            28.06              25.26
  - 600            18.55              16.70
  - 900             6.86               6.18
```

Using forecasting success rates to select bets - figure 47

Selecting Bets using Forecasting Success Rates

match line no. (i)	home odds on coupon (ii)	probability for given odds(%) (iii) P	match points difference (iv) PD	adjusted success rate(%) (v) aSR	include in bet (yes/no) (vi)
1	1/4	80.00	+1200	79.80	no
2	10/11	52.38	+ 600	57.80	Yes
3	6/4	40.00	zero	35.55	no
4	4/5	55.55	+ 300	46.30	no
5	6/5	45.45	+ 300	46.30	Yes
6	11/10	47.62	zero	35.55	no
7	7/2	22.22	- 300	25.26	Yes
8	1/2	66.67	+ 900	66.54	no
9	Evn.	50.00	+ 600	57.80	Yes
10	4/11	73.33	+1200	79.80	Yes
11	1/2	66.67	+ 900	66.54	no
12	5/1	16.67	- 600	16.70	Yes

... etc

If P<aSR then include bet = Yes

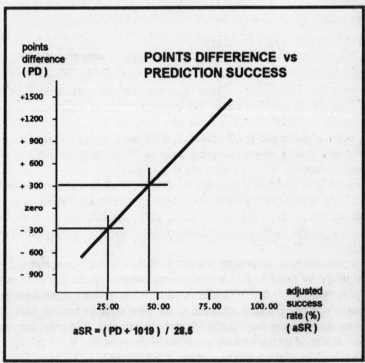

The formula was found to be ....   **aSR = (PD + 1019) / 28.5**

Thus, for *any* value of points difference, the adjusted success rate can easily be found. For example, let the points difference for a match be 1167....

aSR = (1167 + 1019) / 28.5 = 76.70%

If the bookie's probability for this match is less than 76.70%, that is the quoted odds are 1/3, or higher, then the bet should certainly be placed.
Of course similar formulae could be calculated for draw and away forecasts, and there is no reason why all three kinds of forecast should not be combined in a single bet.
The above formula was based upon forecasting success rates derived from

the 'rateform' method (page 12) during a recent football season. The sample size was small. As more data is accumulated the calculations can be re-made. At that stage it may become apparent that the relationship between points difference and success rates is better represented in the form of a 'curve'.

COMPUTER COMPILED ODDS

It is likely that your local betting shop purchases bulk supplies of fixed-odds football coupons. This is probably true of the majority of the independent bookmakers. These coupons may be personalised by the addition of the bookie's name, but coupons found in different shops are frequently identical, with the same odds on offer. Similarly the individual branches of the big three (*Ladbrokes*, *Hills* and *Corals*) are supplied with their own design of pre-compiled coupons. It is apparent that the high street bookmaker is by no means the 'odds-maker'.

You will also find that if coupons from *different* sources are compared the compilers are adopting a very similar approach to the calculation of prices. Indeed, many shops are now willing to accept bets which have been prepared on the coupon of a rival bookmaker, subject of course to their own betting restrictions.

It is probable that the pricing process is, at least in part, computerised, but you would be lucky to find a professional compiler willing to divulge the precise nature of the algorithms used. What follows, therefore, is a *summary* of one possible approach to the generation of betting odds. It is the method used in the *Football Yearbook* software. The odds generated provide a good match with the commercial coupons, and the resulting data can readily be adapted for the purpose of prediction.

A basic understanding of this system requires *no* knowledge of computing or programing.

Many forecasting methods use some kind of 'points difference' rating to predict home, draw and away results. For example, in a typical system, *Rangers* may have accumulated **1400** points and *Celtic* **850**. In such circumstances, with *Rangers* playing at home against *Celtic*, a positive points difference of **550** (1400 minus 850) might suggest a comprehensive home win. Similarly, in another match, a negative difference of, say -600, would indicate an away victory is likely. In such a system any differences between +200 and -200 could suggest a draw. There would also be a small allocation of points to the home team's points total, which reflected the advantage to that team of playing on its own ground.

Such forecasting methods are not easily adapted to the compilation of odds, and, if they are, an extremely thorough and ongoing analysis of forecasting success rates becomes necessary, similar to that described in the previous section.

Goals scored and lost can also form the basis of these calculations, but, whatever the approach, only a time-consuming analysis of prediction success rates, over a prolonged period, can provide sufficient raw material for the calculations.

Fortunately, there is a less complex and more direct solution. The answer is to use a system which computes *statistical probabilities* directly from the proportions of past wins, draws and losses.

As previously discussed, probabilities are based upon past experience, and in their assessment the assumption is made that events will occur in the same proportions in the future as they have in the past.

It might be found that, of all of the games played over a specified period, 45% were home wins, 26% draws and 29% away wins. Values such as these can be converted directly into odds.

The first step in the process is to specify the length of the sequence of matches which will be used to calculate the win, draw and loss ratio.

In preparing the *Yearbook* prediction software it was decided to allow the user some freedom in making this choice. A small number of the most recent matches (for example the last 5 games played) may best reflect the current form of a team, but such a sequence tends to generate some extreme values. These might produce odds which are too generous by far to appear on a fixed-odds coupon. To overcome this difficulty, the program allows the selection of a *specified number* of the most recent matches played but, *in addition*, makes use of the win, draw and losses ratios found in the league division tables (which better reflect long-term form).

These two forms of data ('table' and 'sequence') can be combined in any proportions, at the discretion of the compiler, but for the sake of simplicity are given equal weighting below. Imagine the number of wins, draws and losses for *two opposing teams* in a league **table** to be as follows ...

```
team 1                      team 2
home results                away results
wins    draws  losses       wins    draws   losses
12(hW)  6(hD)  3(hL)        4(aW)   6(aD)   11(aL)
```

In the football match for which odds are to be calculated *team 1* is playing at home and *team 2* is playing away, so the home record of the first team is added to the away record of the second, to give a home, draw, away ratio from the 'table' data of ...

```
home = 23 (hW+aL) = 54.76%
draw = 12 (hD+aD) = 28.57%
away =  7 (hL+aW) = 16.67%
```

90

A similar calculation is carried out using the results from the **five game sequence** leading directly up to the match for which the odds are to be assessed.

This 'sequence' ratio is calculated as follows ...

```
team 1, last 5 home games played (h) = WWWDW
team 2, last 5 away games played (a) = LLLWD

home = 7 (hW+aL) = 70.00%
draw = 2 (hD+aD) = 20.00%
away = 1 (hL+aW) = 10.00%
```

By combining these 'table' and 'sequence' percentage values in *equal* proportions (although this too is at the discretion of the odds compiler) the *ratio* becomes ...

home 62.381%   draw 24.286%   away 13.333%

These are the probabilities which will be converted into odds.

It will be noticed that the results in the 5 match sequence have already been included in the league table record. This is not a problem. The compiler can adjust the relative emphasis towards either recent form or long term form, as thought best.

The league table data (at least in the latter stages of the season) generates a more uniform range of odds, whereas small match sequences can produce extreme values not often encountered on the fixed-odds coupon. Early in the season it makes sense to use *only* the table data. (The match sequence data would simply duplicate that found in the table).

The odds compiler might also decide to use the previous season's league tables when few matches have been played in the current season.

You will notice that by combining the *home* record of the home team with the *away* record of the away team the variable **home advantage** has been taken into account, without the need for further adjustment. (The larger number of home team wins and away team losses ensure that this is so).

The next step is to convert the home, draw and away probabilities to odds. Precisely how this is done is explained on page 73. However the calculation of *betting odds* presents some special problems. Many probabilities (such as, say, a draw at **27.842%**) when first calculated, are not conveniently converted into odds. The answer is to select, from the *traditional* range of betting odds, those *closest* to the calculated probability.

The list in figure 42 shows the relationship between odds, column (i) and, probabilities, column (v). It will be seen that the odds closest to a **27.842%** probability are **13/5**.

Using probabilities, home=62.381%, draw=24.286% and away=13.333%,

which you will recall are calculated *directly* from past
results, the closest probabilities, and hence odds, on
the list can be selected. They are ...

Home 8/13   Draw 3/1   Away 13/2

It should be borne in mind that where the calculated probability is found to
lie between two listed values then adjustments will have to be made to
ensure the sum of the three probabilities remains close to 100%. This is not
difficult to achieve.

As we have seen, odds are compiled by bookmakers in such a way as to
restrict winnings. The nature of the bookie's *profit margin* is explained on
page 77. By increasing the *individual* probability values for homes, draws
and aways, the *sum* of the percentages *exceeds* 100. This excess is
frequently between 10% and 14%, with an average of around 12%.

It can be seen in figure 42 that *increasing* the probability from, say,
16.67% to 20.00%, has the effect of *reducing* the odds from 5/1 to 4/1.

To accurately simulate the bookie's prices it is necessary to include a value
for the over-round. If, for example, 12.00% were chosen, then the home,
draw, and away probabilities of 62.381%, 24.286% and 13.333%,
calculated above, would each be *increased* by that proportion, with the
effect that the complete set of odds would be *shortened* to ...

Home 4/9   Draw 11/4   Away 11/2

Various other adjustments have to be considered. For example,
unacceptable extremes in odds must be avoided. Odds will then more
closely resemble those formulated by the professional compiler.

You will notice that on a fixed-odds coupon the range of odds quoted for
draws is not large. Using a computer program, draw odds can easily be
confined within prescribed limits. Continuing, the odds might become ...

Home 8/15   Draw 5/2   Away 9/2

Although prices may be manipulated in all sorts of ways the values *must*
continue to reflect the *relative abilities* of the opposing teams.

If you own a computer, and have the appropriate software, you will be able
to price a fixture list. Having done so, compare your prices with those
provided by the bookmaker to help identify matches which seem to offer
good value.

*Note : The odds compiler supplied with the Football Yearbook software is
described on page 125, and each step in the process considered in detail.*

SINGLES versus DOUBLES

It is sometimes argued that, in placing a bet, doubles *invariably* produce a superior return to singles.

This is too simplistic a view, for there are many variables to consider, of which one of the most important is the forecasting success rate or 'strike rate'.

Comparing the Return on Singles and Doubles - figure 49

Return on Singles & Doubles for 100 one unit
bets at Evens (1/1) and varying Strike Rates

Success Rates % (i)	Singles Prob. % (ii)	Singles Return in units (iii)	Doubles Prob. % (iv)	Doubles Return in units (v)	Advantage Singles vs Doubles (vi)	Overall Units Gained or Lost on 'best' Bets (vii)
10.0	10.0	20	1.0	4	+16 singles.....loss	-80
20.0	20.0	40	4.0	16	+24 singles.....loss	-60
30.0	30.0	60	9.0	36	+24 singles.....loss	-40
40.0	40.0	80	16.0	64	+16 singles.....loss	-20
50.0	50.0	100	25.0	100	no diference......even	
60.0	60.0	120	36.0	144	+24 doubles.....gain	+44
70.0	70.0	140	49.0	196	+56 doubles.....gain	+96
80.0	80.0	160	64.0	256	+96 doubles.....gain	+156
90.0	90.0	180	81.0	324	+144 doubles.....gain	+224
100.0	100.0	200	100.0	400	+200 doubles.....gain	+300

First of it all should be realised that, for the sake of clarity, the explanation which follows does not consider the effects of betting tax. In practice, a reduction in the strike rate by the current percentage rate of tax, or an equivalent increase in the bookie's 'probability', is a necessity.

With the above stipulation in mind, it can be stated ..... *if the punter can devise a selection strategy where the strike rate is consistently superior to the bookie's odds expressed as a probability then, and only then, are doubles to be preferred to singles.*

Examine figure 49. The table shows the extent to which the return on 100 one unit bets at even odds varies with strike rate and the choice of bet.

Consider the strike rate of **60%** in column *(i)*. The probability of winning with singles is of course **60%** *(col.ii)*, which gives a total return, at odds of **1/1** for 100 bets of one unit, of **120** units *(col.iii)*. Compare this with the probability of a successful double, which is 60% X 60% = **36%** *(col.iv)*. This means that 36 correct doubles returns **144** units *(col.v)*.

The advantage of placing doubles over singles amounts to **24 units** (*col.vi*), and the overall profit on betting *100 doubles* (the 'best' bet) is **44 units** (*col.vii*). However, this assumes a long-term guarantee of successful forecasting in *excess* of 50% at odds of 1/1.

Relating returns to strike rate for singles and doubles - figure 50

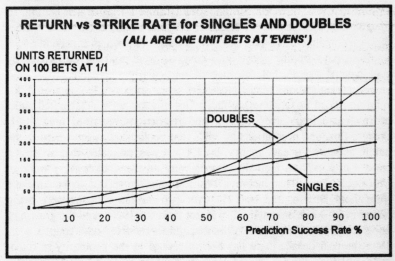

Unfortunate as it may be, the ordinary Joe Punter cannot generally rely upon such a degree of success. Suppose the success rate is only **40%**. Complete the same series of calculations as before. Not only is there an *overall loss* of 20 units on singles, but an even greater loss is incurred by betting doubles (*ie 16 units are saved if the bets are singles*).

If the strike rate *equals* the bookie's probability (in the above example, because odds are 1/1, this is when both are **50%**) singles and doubles give exactly the **same** return and the punter breaks even in the long-term.

Figure 50 summarises the relationship between strike rate, singles and doubles. The lesson is ... the better the strike rate, the better betting doubles. To sum up, if you have developed a winning system, or have considerable confidence in your selections, then bet doubles, or *perhaps* accumulators *. However for the occasional gambler, relying primarily upon 'good luck', potential losses are reduced by betting, whenever possible, on singles.

* Note : If you wish to bet on accumulators the increasingly negative effect of the bookies's profit margin must be considered (page 100).

Fixed-Odds Football Betting

Football gambling began in the 19th century as informal betting on the terraces of football grounds, but it was not until the establishment of regular match fixtures that the opportunity arose for *pre-match* betting. In the 1880s newspapers in the North of England began to offer fixed prizes for correct match forecasts. These prizes became known as 'fixed-odds'.

In those days tipping sheets and coupons were sold on the streets by bookmakers' agents, but, because of particularly restrictive lottery and gambling legislation, many promoters were successfully prosecuted for running illegal prize games. In fact a Government act which banned street betting came into force in 1906, and restrictions remained until 1961. Despite this, and accusations by MP's that bookmakers were whetting the public appetite for easy money, by 1907 it was estimated that at least a quarter of a million football coupons were on the market every week in Liverpool alone. This lucrative business quickly spread to bookmakers throughout Britain, and by 1913 over two million coupons were being issued every week nationally. It was not until the 1920s, and the growth of pools firms, that there was a fall in demand for the fixed-odds coupon.

Over the past decade there has been a revival in the popularity of fixed-odds, although the UK national lottery appears to have brought about a slight, it is hoped temporary, decline in all forms of football betting.

With the belated encouragement of the government, in the form of more liberal legislation, there is now a positive attempt by bookmakers to depart from the somewhat seedy image of the past and to appeal to a wider public. Consequently both local and nationwide bookmakers have begun to provide increasingly attractive and comfortable premises for the use of their clientele. Indeed, goverment legislation introduced in the mid-1990s, which permits longer opening hours and a greater freedom to advertise, should encourage the trend.

It is often said, and undoubtedly true, that there are few poor bookmakers, and of course the *raison d'etre* of the gambling industry is to make money. However punters *do* win, and those with a basic understanding of the nature of probabilities and odds, backed up by a well-structured staking strategy, are undoubtedly best placed to beat the bookie.

This part of *Football Fortunes* deals exclusively with fixed-odds gambling. It might prove useful at this stage, if you have not yet done so, to read the opening pages of the section headed 'Probabilities and Betting Odds'.

PLACING A BET

Bookmakers provide the fixed-odds football coupons from which we make our betting selections.
An extract from a coupon can be seen in figure 51.

Extract from a fixed odds coupon - figure 51

LONG LIST			If Home wins are included minimum FIVE FOLD and Draws or Aways a TREBLE					
Mark 1 for a home win, 2 for an away win, X for a draw								
HOME		DRAW		AWAY				
Evs	Arsenal	2/1	Sheff. Wed.	13/5				
6/4	Man. City	2/1	Tottenham	13/8				
11/8	Sheff.Utd.	9/4	Everton	13/8				
5/4	Derby	9/4	Nottm.For.	7/4				
8/13	Southend	12/5	West Brom	4/1				
4/7	Wolves	12/5	Watford	9/2				
3/1	Barnet	9/4	Port Vale	4/5				
6/5	Wigan	9/4	Torquay	15/8				
1/2	Kettering	12/5	Gateshead	5/1				
11/4	Dundee	9/4	Celtic	5/6				
1/2	Rangers	12/5	Hearts	11/2				
7/4	Clyde	9/4	Dumbarton	5/4				
6/4	Forfar	15/8	Qn.of Sth.	7/4				

One advantage of fixed-odds betting is that it does not suffer from some of the limitations of the football pools, although there remain, as will be seen, a number of restrictions. Nevertheless, a major attraction of this form of gambling is the great diversity of bets which can be placed.... which in turn presents an increased forecasting challenge.

While the return on your investment may be substantially less than that offered by the major pools companies, it is certain that winnings of some kind are going to be much more frequent. Also, unlike football pools, the precise payout on any bet can, without too much difficulty, be calculated in advance. The odds are *fixed* before the match, and normally remain unaltered.

For each match on a fixed-odds coupon the individual odds are expressed for a **home win**, **draw** and **away win**. Consider the following ....

Home	Draw	Away
8/13 *IPSWICH*	**12/5** *OLDHAM*	**4/1**

(On some coupons home and away odds are listed before draws)

In each case the the second figure of the odds value represents the amount to be staked by the punter to win the first. So, a **13 pence** bet on an *Ipswich* home victory would, if successful, *win* **8** pence, and provide a *total return* of **21 pence**... that is winnings *plus* a refund of the stake.

Similarly, **5p** on a draw would return **17p**.

Unfortunately the calculations are not always straightforward.

A £1 bet on a draw, at the above price, would return ....

(£1 X 12) / 5 = £2.40 + £1 (refunded stake) = £3.40
(In these examples betting tax has not been considered)

You can read more concerning the calculation of winnings on page 77.

When the time comes to make your match selections, annotate the fixed-odds coupon with a **'1'** for a HOME win, an **'X'** for a DRAW and a **'2'** for an AWAY win. In doing so, it makes good sense to place all of your forecasts on the 'Long List', where you are allowed the fullest choice of matches *(see 'Betting Strategy', page 100)*. Note that the 'Long List' is sometimes called the 'Nothing Barred List'.

The single bet, on *one* result, is frequently the best bet. Other wagers are designed to generate a larger return from a small outlay by multiplying odds together.... but with more match selections the chances of success are reduced. Also, with more matches in a bet, the profit taken by the bookie has an increasingly adverse effect upon the return *(figure 54, page 101)*.

Unfortunately, whatever your wishes, it is not always possible to bet on a single result. 'Singles' are currently restricted to televised and 'cup' matches. Indeed, a minimum of five matches must often be included in your bet if it includes a home prediction; while aways and draws are commonly restricted to no less than three selections. The bookie may also stipulate a *maximum* number of draw selections.

It is the client's responsibility to be aware of betting restrictions, or risk a wager being declared void.

The reality is that most of your bets will consist of three matches (*a treble*) or more, and *fully multiplied odds* (**FMO**) will apply. In such bets the *return* from *each* correct selection becomes the *stake* for the next.

Take this example of a successful treble. The odds offered by the bookie for the three matches you wish to select as away wins happen to be **2/1, 5/2** and **Evens**. In *one column* of the Long List you will mark **'2'** against each of your three selections, and annotate the coupon **"£1 Treble"**.

The bet *(ignoring tax)* costs £1, and the return of £21, for a successful wager, is calculated as follows ...

£1 at 2/1 gives ... (£1 X 2) / 1 = £2 + stake = £3

This £3 becomes the 'stake' for the second selection

£3 at 5/2 gives ... (£3 X 5) / 2 = £7.50 + £3 = £10.50

Finally calculate the return on £10.50 at 'evens' (1/1)

£10.50 at 1/1 gives .. (£10.50 X 1) / 1 = £10.50 + £10.50 = £21.00

There is a more efficient way to make such calculations. Consider odds of **2/5, 4/7, 1/4** and **11/5** in a *fourfold* (4 selections). From *each* of the odds values create a fraction. This fraction consists of the sum of the component values of the odds placed over the value to the right of the odds ....

2/5 becomes (2 + 5) / 5 = 7/5
4/7 becomes (4 + 7) / 7 = 11/7   etc ...

Calculate the product of these fractions and the stake to find the return ....

7/5 X 11/7 X 5/4 X 16/5 = 44/5 = 8.8
£1 bet returns £1 X 8.8 = £8.80 *(includes refunded stake)*

Invariably you will carry out such calculations *before* placing a bet, to re-assure yourself that you are making a a worthwhile investment.

The onus is upon you to be sure that the bet is accurately described on the fixed-odds coupon. The preceding wager was simply a **"£1 fourfold"**, however many bets are much more complex and take the form of 'mathematical combinations'. These are generally *(and incorrectly)* referred to, in the world of gambling, as **permutations**.

Here is an example. If *four* coupon selections are made, they can be arranged in such a way as to provide **four trebles**.

98

Suppose that the four match lines you select are numbered **12, 13, 17** and **20** on the coupon.

Treble bets can be formed as follows ...

12,13,17   12,13,20   12,17,20   and   **13,17,20**

Perm 3 from 4 aways - figure 52

pswich	12/5			
an. City	11/5			
oventry	2/1			
heff Utd	9/4	2		
.P.R.	11/5	2		
rsenal	12/5			
ldham	12/5			
imbledon	3/1			
iddlesbro	13/5	2		
atford	5/2			
est Ham	11/5			
ristol C.	12/5	2		
outhend	5/2			

Perm 3 from 4 aways gives 4 trebles at £1 = £4

Any of the four sets of three matches correctly predicted and the payout is for *one* treble. All four forecasts correct and you are paid for *four* trebles.

If you decide to bet £1 per treble, then mark the coupon ....

    "Perm 3 from 4 = 4 lines at £1 = £4"

A bet of this kind is shown in figure 52. Notice that the word 'line' in football betting is often synonymous with 'bet'. In the above entry there are

4 'match selections' in a single column. The wager consists of 4 lines (4 trebles).
Alternatively, the instructions with these four match selections might have been ...

"Perm 3 from 4, plus 1 fourfold = 5 lines at £1 = £5"

There are now five bets. The total stake is £5. Four correct away predictions and the bookie would pay out for 4 trebles and 1 four match accumulator. When placing such bets any number of matches can be selected, and all sorts of permutations included, provided no individual line is outwith the bookmaker's betting restrictions.

Numbers of doubles, trebles & accumulators - figure 53

Matches:	2	3	4	5	6	7	8	9	10
Dbls	1	3	6	10	15	21	28	36	45
Tbls		1	4	10	20	35	56	84	120
4			1	5	15	35	70	126	210
5				1	6	21	56	126	252
6					1	7	28	84	210
7						1	8	36	120
8							1	9	45
9								1	10
Total Bets	1	4	11	26	57	120	247	502	1013

Of course it is important to be sure that the number of bets in each permutation, and the total number of bets submitted, are correctly calculated .... figure 53 will help. Using this table, if you were to select **six matches**, and then place a bet consisting of **20 trebles, 15 fourfolds, 6 fivefolds, and 1 six match accumulator**, the total number of bets is **42**. You will find that that fourfolds, fivefolds, etc, are sometimes referred to as 4 timers, 5 timers, and so on.

Some examples of coupon entries are provided a little later in this book.

To quickly and accurately determine the payout for many of your wagers an electronic calculator, or computer software, is a must.

BETTING STRATEGY

In placing a bet use the 'Long List' or the 'Correct Scores List'. It is best to ignore all others. For example the 'Sections List', in which the bookmaker *groups* matches of his own choosing, should be avoided. The individual odds on offer for each match are invariably no better than those on the 'Long List'. The aim of lists of this kind is to entice the punter into making poor betting decisions.

The fixed-odds punter will frequently try to identify the 'best' or *banker* predictions from the matches on the 'Long List'. Always use your own system, or computer software, to make such choices. Do *not* simply select the matches which offer the shortest odds and treat them as bankers. There is no evidence whatsoever that the 'form' selections of the bookmaker are in any way superior to the selections you might make through the use of a good forecasting system of your own choosing.

Merely accepting the bookie's ratings places you at an immediate disadvantage. You are reducing the potential return at one stroke. The bookmaker is not, after all, making money through a superior ability to predict results. It is by offering less than statistically fair odds (page 77).

Doubles and trebles *may* produce a superior return to singles (page 92), but it does make sense to keep the total number of match selections in a multiple bet (an 'accumulator') within reasonable bounds. There are two reasons for this. First of all, you will notice in figure 8, on page 17, that there is a close correlation between prediction ratings and success rates. Correct forecasts quickly 'fall-off' as form rating values decrease.

There is a second reason for keeping down the size of accumulators. This is a direct consequence of the effects of the bookie's over-round. You will find that the *average* multiplied odds offered by a bookmaker for a draw treble are about **33/1**; whereas the *fair* odds for such a bet should be closer to **60/1**. Similarly, the fully multiplied odds for a fivefold of draw forecasts come to about **360/1**; but *without* the inclusion of the bookie's profit margin this would be in the region of **1250/1**.

The problem is clearly illustrated in figure 54. The true odds for the occurrence of a particular result might be **9/4**; but include the bookie's over-round and the odds actually offered to the punter are reduced to **15/8**. Use both of these prices in a series of accumulators and compare the profit from a successful bet. It becomes clear just how much is being withheld by the bookmaker; and it can be seen that the percentage loss to the punter increases dramatically with the number of matches in the bet.

To help redress the balance a little compare the odds quoted by different bookmakers for the same series of matches. Several papers, the *Racing*

Post, Sporting Life, RaceForm Update, etc, analyse
odds from different sources and identify the best value.
Of course it is inevitable that if you are betting on the
most fancied outcome of a match the odds will be poor.

Fair odds versus bookie's odds in accumulators - figure 54

```
Comparing returns on bets using 'fair' odds
and 'bookie's' odds.  The Stake is £1
```

type of bet	bookies odds of 15/8 profit(£)	fair odds of 9/4 profit(£)	loss of profit(£)	loss as percent.
single	1.88	2.25	0.37	16.44%
double	7.27	9.56	2.29	23.95%
treble	22.76	33.33	10.57	31.71%
4 fold	67.32	110.57	43.25	39.11%
5 fold	195.42	361.59	166.17	45.95%
6 fold	563.71	1,177.42	613.71	52.12%
7 fold	1,622.55	3,828.87	2,206.32	57.62%
8 fold	4,666.70	12,446.06	7,779.36	62.50%
9 fold	13,418.63	40,451.95	27,033.32	66.83%
10 fold	38,580.45	131,471.00	92,890.55	70.65%

There is then pressure to select a larger number of matches to achieve a
satisfactory return on your money. However, careful scrutiny of football
coupons may identify value bets, where extra-generous odds seem to have
been quoted by the bookie. Securing the best odds will go some way to help
reduce the size of multiple bets.

The over-riding lesson is to bet on *sound information*. In doing so you are
trying to find 'value' from the bookmaker. This means identifying situations
where the bookmaker appears to have underestimated the probability of an
event and looks to be paying 'over the odds'.

Remember value for money does not necessarily mean selecting long odds.
Value bets could be odds on ! To this end you could try to develop a system
which analyses past prediction success rates; then applies the results of the
anaysis to the selection of matches. Such an approach has been described
on page 84.

Finally, it is worth bearing in mind that the fixed-odds coupon is prepared
five or six days in advance of play. This confers a slight advantage on the
punter who may be able to refer to more recent 'intelligence'.

KEEPING RECORDS

It is advisable to maintain a full record of betting costs and returns.... without doing so it is easy to gain a false impression of the size of cumulative wins or losses.

It is also makes sense to establish just how much you are prepared to risk, and perhaps lose, over a specified period.

The punter may be keen to invest winnings in future bets. Here is one way to achieve this, while, at the same time, controlling the total amount spent.

To begin with, you must decide upon the total number of bets to be placed. This might be one bet each week over a twenty week period. Put aside a 'bank', say £20, and then bet as follows ...

```
Week 1 : Bank = £20.00
Stake = £20.00 / 20 = £1.00
Wins at 3/1    Return = £4.00    Bank = £23.00

Week 2 : Bank = £23.00   Stake = £23.00 / 19 = £1.21
Loses this week so Bank = £21.79

Week 3 : Bank = £21.79   Stake = £21.79 / 18 = £1.21
Wins at 9/2    Return = £6.65    Bank = £27.23   etc ....
```

Continue over the full twenty weeks.

All winnings are placed in the bank and are used to increase the stake for the subsequent bet. It is an easy matter to keep track of your failures and successes over the specified period.

You will find that the 'Greenwood System', on page 109, provides a more sophisticated approach to managing your bets. It is a system which takes betting tax into consideration, and guarantees a profit if modest forecasting standards are achieved.

ANTE-POST BETTING

The bookie will provide the opportunity to place a wager upon an event some time before it occurs; perhaps as much as a year in advance.

The lure of such bets is the seemingly attractive odds. However, in truth, the odds are attractive only to the bookmaker !

For example, consider odds offered by a bookmaker for a moderately skilled football team about to play in a cup competition. To win the competition the team must be victorious in at least six successive matches. The bookie quotes odds of **21/1** for the team to take the trophy.

The reality is that to achieve fully multiplied odds of 21/1 over six games the 'average' odds for each match amount to a mere **4/6**. This is regardless of the quality of the opposition or whether matches are played at home or

away.
Effectively, for every game played by a rather mediocre team, the probabilty of a win is considerably less than even, and the team *must* win all six matches before any winnings can be collected. The odds of 4/6 are those which might normally be quoted for a top team playing at home. You would be better advised to place a series of singles. The ante-post bet fills the pockets of the bookmaker whilst providing excellent publicity. It is not recommended.

BETTING TAX

Deal with betting tax as follows. You will see that in these examples the tax rate is 10%.... but please see the note at the foot of the page.

Prepayment

When *placing your bet* with a bookmaker make a payment to the bookmaker of 10% of the sum staked.
For example with odds of 5/1 and £10 staked ....

> **Pay the bookie the £10 wager, plus 10% = £11.00**
> **Receive £60.00 when you win. The profit is £49.00**

Post-payment

Place the bet of £10 at 5/1 but with no additional payment.
If you win the bookie deducts 10% *before payout* ....

> **Pay the bookie £10.00 for the wager**
> **Receive £60.00 less 10% tax = £54.00   The profit is £44.00**

Although the *prepayment* profit is greater, don't forget that you *pay* the bookie 10% more than you do on *afterpayment*.
If you were to place a post-paid bet, but increase your initial wager by 10%, the loss in profit is much reduced. With the same odds of 5/1 ....

> **Pay the bookie £11.00 as a wager (*ie increase the wager by 10%*)**
> **Receive £66 less 10% tax = £59.40   The profit is £48.40**

Note : In March 1996, after many years without change, the tax rate was reduced from 10% to 9%. The Government has intimated that there may be further reductions. For this reason, and the sake of clarity in these and subsequent examples, a 10% tax rate has been applied.

104

BETS USING THE LONG LIST

There follows a description of some bets you might decide to place with your local bookmaker

These examples show selections, coupon annotations, and the payout for a stated number of correct predictions.

HOMES, DRAWS or AWAYS

Here are three basic bets which could be entered on the long list.

An 'odds calculator' has been used to compute the payout.

```
EIGHT HOMES - ACCUMULATORS

 3  Swansea      home win      6 folds  = 28
 7  Grimsby      home win      7 folds  =  8
18  Oxford       home win      8 folds  =  1
25  Barnet       home win      Total Bets = 37
42  Welling      home win      at 10p per line
45  Dunfermline  home win      costs £3.70
49  East Fife    home win      Total Cost £4.07
53  Alloa        home win      ( with 10% tax )
```

PAYOUT for eight homes with 7 of 8 correct and odds of
  8/15 10/11 4/7 11/10 10/11 5/6 6/4

```
6 folds  = 7    Pays £31.76
7 folds  = 1    Pays £8.45

Total £40.21  ( tax pre-paid )
```

*With the eighth result correct at odds of 4/7,
this bet would have paid £183.49*

```
SIX DRAWS - TREBLES

 8  Luton v Watford    draw    Treble(s)  = 20
20  Plymouth v Cardiff draw    Total Bets = 20
21  Rotherham v Hull   draw    Total Cost = £2
34  Lincoln Preston    draw     at 10p per line
50  Morton Stirling    draw    ( no tax paid )
56  Montrose Forfar    draw
```

PAYOUT for six draws with only 4 of 6 correct
and odds of 2/1 9/4 13/5 5/2

```
Treble(s) = 4  Pays £14.80
Total return £13.32 ( with 10% tax deducted )
```

*With the two additional results correct at odds of 9/4 each,
this bet would have paid out £65.04*

SIX AWAYS - ACCUMULATORS

14	Charlton	away win
24	Bradford	away win
30	Doncaster	away win
44	Raith Rov	away win
47	Hamilton	away win
50	Dumbarton	away win

5 folds   = 6
6 folds   = 1
Total Bets = 7
Cost £0.77
at 10p per line
(with 10% tax)

PAYOUT for six aways with 5 of 6 correct
and odds of 9/5 2/1 5/4 1/1 8/11

5 folds = 1 Pays £6.53
Total £6.53   (tax pre-paid)

*With the sixth result correct at odds of 5/4,
this bet would have paid out £53.74*

FOUR AWAYS with BANKERS

Pick your best two aways as *bankers (which must be correctly forecast)* and
six other likely aways.　　　Annotate your coupon as shown in figure 55.

**Four aways
with bankers
- figure 55**

With average
odds of 6/4 and
both bankers
correct this
would pay
(*after tax*)
as follows ....

**2 others
correct
pays £35**

**3 others
correct
pays £105**

**4 others
correct
pays £210**

pswich	12/5	2	B	
an. City	11/5			
oventry	2/1	2		
heff Utd	9/4			
.P.R.	11/5	2	B	
rsenal	12/5	2		
ldham	12/5			
imbledon	3/1	2		
iddlesbro	13/5	2		
atford	5/2			
est Ham	11/5			
ristol C.	12/5	2		
outhend	5/2	2		

**Perm 2 bankers (B)
with any 2 from 6 gives
15 fourfolds at £1 = £15**

FIVE HOMES PLANNED ENTRY

The layout of a 'planned entry' on a fixed-odds coupon provides certain guarantees on the return, depending upon the number of errors made in your predictions. This first example uses **ten home win selections** arranged in **six columns**, as shown in figure 56.

Five homes planned entry - figure 56

	col 1	col 2	col 3	col 4	col 5	col 6
1		1		1	1	
2	1			1	1	
3		1	1		1	
4	1		1			1
5		1		1		1
6	1			1	1	
7		1	1		1	
8	1		1			1
9		1		1		1
10	1		1			1
	50p	50p	50p	50p	50p	50p

For convenience, the match lines are numbered 1 to 10, but of course you would make your 10 selections from the total number of matches on the Long List. All selections should provide odds of **4/6** or higher.

Referring to figure 56, enter '1', for your first home win selection, in columns 2, 4 and 5. Next, place your second home selection in columns 1, 4 and 5. Continue until the layout in the above figure is complete.

If the coupon's Long List does not have six columns, try making use of columns in an adjacent list, or simply use an additional coupon.

Enter an identical stake at the foot of each column. In the example the stake for each bet is 50p, giving a total cost of £3.00. Each bet is a fivefold. With **eight** correct forecasts you are virtually sure to *double* your total stake, while with **nine** right you will get back *six times* your total stake.

Even with seven right you still have a 50% chance of doubling your total stake.

THREE AWAYS PLANNED ENTRY

Once again the layout of the planned entry provides certain guarantees. This second example covers **eight away selections** arranged in **seven columns**, as shown in figure 57.

Choose eight aways with odds of **6/4** or higher

Referring to figure 57, enter '2', for your first away win selection, in columns 1 and 4. Next, place your second away selection in columns 2, 3 and 5. Continue until the layout in the figure is complete.

If the coupon's Long List does not have seven columns, try making use of columns in an adjacent list, or simply use an additional coupon.

Enter an identical stake at the foot of each column. In the example the stake for each bet is 50p, giving a total cost of £3.50. Each bet is a treble.

Three aways planned entry - figure 57

	col 1	col 2	col 3	col 4	col 5	col 6	col 7
1	2			2			
2		2	2		2		
3	2				2	2	
4	2	2					2
5				2			2
6		2	2			2	
7				2		2	
8			2		2		2
	50p	50p	50p	50p	50p	50p	50p

With **five** correct forecasts you are almost sure to *double* your total stake. With **six** correct you will certainly get back *four* times your total stake, with a 40% chance of getting back six times your total stake. Even with just four right there is a 50% chance of doubling your total stake

---

THE PRINCIPLE OF THE PLANNED ENTRY

Two 'planned entries' have just been described. They are often known as 'guarantee blocks'. When constructing entries of this kind it is necessary to decide the following ....

1. **The total number of matches to be used.**
2. **The number of matches in each bet** *(ie matches in each column).* For example, five matches were in the homes planned entry and three matches in the aways planned entry, just described.
3. **The margin of error permissible** *(ie incorrect predictions).*

Suppose the idea is to cover **6 away wins** in groups (ie columns) of *three*, so that any **4** correct will guarantee a winning treble.

As there are 6 matches covered 3 at a time, there will be three empty spaces in each column. Two errors are permissible from these six selections.

These two errors can occur in **15** ways in 6 matches.

1	1	1	1	1	2	2	2	2	3	3	3	4	4	5
2	3	4	5	6	3	4	5	6	4	5	6	5	6	6

The 'error doubles' shown above must be accomodated within the 3 empty spaces in each column. Three doubles can be placed in three empty spaces.

eg The 'empty spaces' treble $\begin{smallmatrix}2\\5\\6\end{smallmatrix}$ will take care of error doubles $\begin{smallmatrix}2\\5\end{smallmatrix}$ | $\begin{smallmatrix}2\\6\end{smallmatrix}$ | $\begin{smallmatrix}5\\6\end{smallmatrix}$

In this example it might be expected that the 15 error doubles could fit exactly into 5 empty spaces provided by five columns.

In fact six columns are necessary (and hence six trebles) to accomodate all 15 error doubles. In figure 58A, the 18 errors (represented by 'E') have been placed in six columns to cover the necessary 15 error doubles.

The blank spaces (represented by 'o') are then replaced by away win entries to arrive at figure 58B, the final planned entry.

	'A'					
1	o	o	E	o	E	E
2	E	E	o	o	o	E
3	o	o	E	E	o	E
4	o	E	o	E	E	o
5	E	o	o	E	E	o
6	E	E	E	o	o	o

	'B'					
1	2	2		2		
2				2	2	2
3	2	2			2	
4	2		2			2
5		2	2			2
6				2	2	2

The 'GREENWOOD'

The 'Greenwood', named after its originator, is a **five homes staking
system,** for betting on fixed-odds coupons. It *guarantees* a profit within a
month if you can achieve a *20%* forecasting success rate.

The system depends on two things. Your ability to correctly forecast five
home wins from the full Nothing Barred List once in five attempts, and the
financial resources to sustain a moderately long losing run.

Given these, and the patience to wait several weeks for success, you could
well end the season with a handsome profit.

How *much* profit will be made depends upon your forecasting ability and
the size of your **'target'** figure (the amount you require as clear profit when
you ultimately win).

The system guarantees that when a win occurs, you will receive, after tax, a
sum comprising *all* previous losses, the *return* of the current week's stake,
plus your target payout.

It is possible to pick home wins of any odds, but advisable to select from a
range of approximately **1/3** to **4/5**. The *fully multiplied odds* (FMO) are
then **8 to 1**, or thereabouts (see page 97). Any shorter odds and the losses
will build up too quickly for comfort.

Let us suppose that the first week's selections have FMO of **7.8 to 1**.

Multiply this by **0.9** (to allow for the betting tax) then subtract **1** (to cover your stake) ....

$$7.8 \times 0.9 = 7.02 - 1 = 6.02$$

Suppose your target is £25.

Divide £25 by **6.02** to obtain the *stake* for *week 1* ....

$$£25.00 / 6.02 = £4.16$$

If you *win* in week 1 you get back back £29.20. This is, roughly, your stake *plus* your target.

If you *lose*, (the position in the first line of figure 59), select another five homes the following week.

The 'Greenwood' system - figure 59

```
Target Win = £25.00
```

Wk	Required Win(£)	FMO (to 1)	Divisor	Weekly Stake(£)	Aggregate Losses(£)
1	25.00	7.80	6.02	4.16	4.16
2	29.16	8.10	6.29	4.64	8.80
3	33.80	7.95	6.15	5.50	14.30
4	39.30	8.30	6.47	6.08	20.38
5	45.38	8.00	6.20	7.32	27.70

In the *second* week the hypothetical FMO are **8.1 to 1**.

Once again multiply the FMO by **0.9** and deduct **1** ...

$$8.1 \times 0.9 = 7.29 - 1 = 6.29$$

However, on this occasion, you want to win your target *plus* the *previous week's losses*, a total of £29.16.

So divide £29.16 by **6.29** for the *week 2 stake* of £4.64.

This procedure is repeated each week until you win. Every week you are attempting to win the target plus your aggregate losses.

If, as suggested, you try to achieve FMO of about **8 to 1**, the stake will increase by a modest **16%** per week.

However, be warned, if you fail to win in five attempts, it may be time to re-assess your forecasting system, or simply cut your losses and stop.

Certainly, if you go on, and eventually win, you will regain your losses and obtain your target.

For example, if it were to take ten weeks, you would be about £86.50 out of pocket before winning back your money, plus the £25 profit. Your stake on that tenth week would be about £15.50.

The above description relates to bets where tax is postpaid.
If you use the *prepayment* method, subtract **1.1** from the FMO.
For example, to calculate the stake in week 1 ....

7.8 - 1.1 = 6.7   £25 / 6.7 = £3.73 (plus tax of 0.37p) = £4.10
If you win this returns £3.73 X 7.8 = £29.10

Note : Apply this system to any form of single bet, and to certain multiple bets, if each part of such a bet is of equal odds.

The 'LUCKY THIRTEEN' Aways Staking Plan

This is simply the above described 'Greenwood' plan adapted for **three aways** and guaranteeing a win within a month with a *20%* forecasting success rate. This method also uses postpaid tax.

This system is based on matches with average away win odds of 6/4, which are usually plentiful on the fixed-odds coupon.

Decide on your target figure, for example £30.00.
To obtain the first week's stake divide by 'lucky thirteen' ....

£30.00 / 13 = £2.31 *(stake rounded up to the next penny)*

Enter three **2's** on the Long List with the stake at the foot of the column.
Should the first bet fail, go for your target plus accrued losses.
This gives a stake for the second week of ....

£32.31 / 13 = £2.49

Carry on until you win.

Figure 60 makes it quite clear. No matter when you win, you will receive your target plus the current stake and all previous losing stakes.

Stakes rise gradually, by just under **8%** a week, so it won't strain your pocket.

Should it be *week 9* before you win you will have expended about £28.50 before regaining this amount and your £30 target.

The 'Lucky Thirteen' staking plan - figure 60

Wk	Required Sum(£)	Stake Sum/13(£)	Accrued Losses(£)
1	30.00	2.31	2.31
2	32.31	2.49	4.80
3	34.80	2.68	7.48
4	37.80 etc...		

Of course, if you wish to use selections with shorter odds, there is no problem. Just work out the fully multiplied odds, multiply by **0.9** and subtract **1**. Then divide the amount you want to win by this value to find the necessary stake.

For example, **10/11**, **5/4** and **6/4** will yield a divisor of **8.66**.

£30.00 divided by **8.66** = **£3.47**, which will return **£33.52** after tax.

The '12X' Plan

This is a plan for the Long List. It covers **homes**, **aways** and **draws**.

Decide on the matches you wish to include in your bet.

Your selections must consist of ....

5 homes with odds of 1/2 or more
3 aways with odds of 6/4 or more
3 draws with odds of 11/5 or more

Enter the 5 homes in the first column.

The 3 aways in the second column.

The 3 draws in the third column.

The same match cannot appear in more than one column.

Annotate the coupon with the following instructions ....

> *"Perm any 4 homes with any 2 aways with any 1 draw.*
> *5 X 3 X 3 = 45 bets at ..... "*

Each bet is a 7 match accumulator.

This plan allows a margin of error in *each* column. There can be one incorrect home, one incorrect away, and two incorrect draws.

The *minimum win* will guarantee to **double** your money.

THREE DRAWS CYCLIC PERMS (example 1)

Select **7 draws**.

Mark **three columns** with headings **A**, **B**, and **C**.

Put **3** draws in column **A**.

2 draws in column **B**.

2 draws in column **C**.

Write instructions as shown in figure 61

**Three draws cyclic perm
(example 1) - figure 61**

A	B	C	
			perm 2 from column A with one from column B
	X		perm 2 from column B with one from column C
X			perm 2 from column C with one from column A
		X	plus column A
X			
	X		Gives 12 trebles at ….
X			
		X	

4 draws guarantees a winning treble with a **37%** chance of *two* winning trebles. **5** draws guarantees at least **3** winning trebles.

THREE DRAWS CYCLIC PERM (example 2)

This time select **8 draws**.

Mark **three columns** on the coupon as **A**, **B**, and **C**.

Put **3** draws in column **A**

3 draws in column **B**

2 draws in column **C**

Write instructions as shown in figure 62.

4 draws guarantees a winning treble,
with a **50%** chance of at least two winning trebles.

5 draws guarantees three winning trebles,
with a **70%** chance of 4 or more winning trebles.

Three draws
cyclic perm
(*example 2*)
- figure 62

A	B	C
	X	
X		
		X
X		
	X	
		X

perm 2 from column A with one from column B

perm 2 from column B with one from column C

perm 2 from column C with one from column A

plus columns A and B

Gives 20 trebles at ....

CORRECT SCORES BETTING

The Correct Scores List is rather different from others. You will find that the odds for each score you might wish to predict vary in *direct relation* to the odds given for homes, draws and aways on the Long List.

Use the table in figure 63, extracted from a coupon, to see how this works.

For example, if on the Long List, the match odds for the **home win** in which you are interested are **10/11**, find this value in the column headed 'Team Odds'. Decide the score by which you think the team will win, say **2-1**, and find this below 'WIN SCORE'. At the point where line and column intersect is the price for your correct score forecast. In this case **15/2**. This table is used to identify both home win and away win score odds. There is another list for draw score odds.

The most prevalent scores are **0-0**, **1-1**, **1-0** and **2-1** (see figure 18).

The odds for all scores predictions are high when compared with other coupon lists. This reflects the greater difficulty of forecasting scores. Nevertheless, the prices quoted fall well short of 'fair' odds, as the bookie's

over-round may be as much as 40% (figure 43).
There are few restrictions on the number of permitted
selections. There follow some examples of score bets.

Correct score win odds - figure 63

Team Odds	WIN SCORE					
	1-0	2-0	2-1	3-0	3-1	3-2
4/5	6	7	15/2	12	10	14
5/6	6	15/2	15/2	14	11	14
10/11	6	15/2	15/2	16	12	16
Evs.	6	8	8	16	12	16
11/10	6	8	8	18	14	16
6/5	6	8	8	20	14	16
5/4	6	9	8	20	16	16

Pick any score for three matches.

match 1	1-0	Three doubles and one
match 2	0-0	treble gives 4 bets at ...
match 3	1-1	

2 correct scores gives one winning double.
All three correct gives 3 doubles and 1 treble.

This time use two different scores for each match line.

match 1	1-0, 1-1	12 doubles
match 2	1-1, 2-1	and 8 trebles
match 3	0-0, 1-0	gives 20 bets at ...

1 correct score in any two matches gives one winning double.
1 correct in all three matches gives 3 doubles and 1 treble.

Select three games that look like low-scoring home wins and cover the best (in the example match 2) with scores of 1-0 and 2-1.
The others are predicted as 1-0, 2-1 and 1-1.

```
match 1  1-0  2-1  1-1
match 2  1-0  2-1              21 doubles at ...
match 3  1-0  2-1  1-1
```

With a correct score in each of any two lines, you have a win double returning at least 37/1 nett of tax to your unit stake. With a correct score in all three lines, you will have three doubles returning about 117/1 nett of tax to your unit stake.

This time select four games. Cover the most likely home win (in this example match no.3) with score predictions of 1-0 and 2-1. The others are predicted as 1-0, 2-1 and 1-1.

```
match 1  1-0  2-1  1-1
match 2  1-0  2-1  1-1        81 trebles at ...
match 3  1-0  2-1
match 4  1-0  2-1  1-1
```

With a correct score in each of any three lines, you have a win treble returning about 246/1 nett of tax to your unit stake. With a correct score in all four lines, you have four such trebles returning about 1041/1 nett of tax to the unit stake.

The 'BONANZA' Correct Scores Staking Plan

Just like the 'Greenwood' plan on page 109, this plan guarantees to achieve your **target**, plus any accrued losses, but this time allows a *20% margin for error*, as well as an *alternative prediction* for each match.

Select five likely low-score home wins and place an entry as shown below.
If *four* of the matches end **1-0** or **2-1**, you have a winner.
For simplicity use postpaid tax.

Col.1	Col.2	
1-0	2-1	
1-0	2-1	*"Perm 80 fourfolds at .....*
1-0	2-1	*(2 X 2 X 2 X 2 X 5) = £ ..... "*
1-0	2-1	
1-0	2-1	

This system operates as follows.
Decide your target, say **£100.00**. This is the amount you want to win.

To determine the stake, divide the target by **2,080** and then round up the result to the nearest penny ....

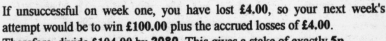

£100 / 2080 = 4.8p, rounded up to 5p

Your entry would read ....

"Perm 80 fourfolds at 5p = £4.00"

If unsuccessful on week one, you have lost £4.00, so your next week's attempt would be to win £100.00 plus the accrued losses of £4.00.
Therefore, divide £104.00 by **2080**. This gives a stake of exactly **5p**.
This means that on week two your bet is once again **80 fourfolds at 5p**.
Continue as shown in figure 64

The 'Bonanza' correct score staking plan - figure 64

	Required Sum (£)	Unit Stake	Total Stake (£)	Accrued Losses (£)
Week				
1	100.00	5p	4.00	4.00
2	104.00	5p	4.00	8.00
3	108.00	6p	4.80	12.80
4	112.80 etc..			

It so happens that because of the high odds and the need to bet in whole pence, by rounding up, on some weeks there is no need to increase the stake. For the same reasons, you are likely to clear a few more pounds than your intended target when you win.
Follow the same procedure each week, till you win.
Note that the value of the divisor, 2080, is determined by the odds offered for scores of 1-0 and 2-1, and the current rate of tax.
If there is insufficient space on the Correct Scores List, use an adjacent list and cross out headings. Alternatively use a betting slip.

Forth Dimension
26 Macbeth Road
Dunfermline.
KY11 4EG

Many of the bets listed in Football Fortunes have been provided by my associate Michael Greenwood. who is prepared to share his experience of football betting. So, if you have any questions concerning the listed examples, or have any other queries about fixed-odds betting, then just write to 'Forth Dimension' and your correspondence will be forwarded.

Football Forecasting and Computing

A great deal can be achieved using pencil and paper. The raw material you need is provided in newspapers and other publications. It is possible to gather data and develop simple forecasting systems manually.

Even so, to fully consider a large number of variables, and to experiment with different prediction techniques, there can be no substitute for a computerised system. So what alternatives are open to the computer owner ? They may be summarised as follows .....

1. **Use one of the many commercial database packages such as dBASE, Access, Paradox, etc.**

2. **Write and develop your own software using languages such as Visual Basic or the *Microsoft* Access database.**

3. **Obtain software 'dedicated' to the purpose of football results forecasting, such as *Forth Dimension's* Football Yearbook.**

In practice the commercial database tends to be insufficiently versatile for the needs of the soccer enthusiast and results forecaster. So, if the requirement is for more than a database, a programming language provides the greatest freedom of design and is a superior option for fine tuning or adding new features. If you should decide to develop your own software the home computer user need look no further than BASIC.

The BASIC language is the best of all of the general-purpose languages.

It is still the easiest to learn, and is ideally suited to the beginner. Of the many BASIC compilers available, *PowerBASIC* for DOS applications, and *Visual Basic* for *Windows,* provide excellent value. Towards the end of this book you will find a BASIC code listing which generates mathematical combinations and is suitable for inclusion in your own applications.

Unfortunately, a fully operational prediction system requires many months, if not years, of development. This means the majority of computer users will go for the third of the above options and purchase dedicated commercial software which incorporates all of the desired features.

PREDICTION SOFTWARE

Take extreme care over the selection of prediction software.

There is much to be expected from a good quality forecasting package.

Use this as a check list ....

Ideally the program will provide a variety of features which will appeal both to the soccer statistician *and* to those whose interest is results forecasting.

League tables and results should be included for the major English and Scottish divisions, plus the minor divisions regularly found on football coupons.

Supplied with up-to-date data for the current football season.

Data covering at least the past ten years, with options for the soccer enthusiast to obtain results and tables over a longer period.

Featuring both football pools and fixed-odds betting.

Offering a variety of forecasting options, including scope to experiment with different prediction settings or parameters.

Statistical analysis of forecasting success rates.

Rapid and efficient update with the latest match results, including an option to add current fixture lists to facilitate results input.

Text and graphics displays which can be printed, or copied to other applications such as word processors, spreadsheets and so on.

Low cost 'update service', either by post or through e-mail.

Supplier to provide annual upgrades including new features.

Telephone or e-mail technical support and advice.

Competitive selling price.

Here are some further examples of what a good prediction program should provide. The displays have been extracted from the *Yearbook* software.

Inputting Results

In the past the input of match results has been regarded as a major bugbear. This is no longer the case. Your software supplier should be prepared to offer regular updates of results and tables, by post or e-mail, at a minimal cost. Even so, with a modern system, and a mouse, the user should expect to be able to input a full week's league results within thirty minutes.

In figure 65, a *Windows*™ interface, all input operations are achieved using a mouse, without the need to touch a keyboard ! The user can enter team names, goals scored, fixture lists, matches from coupons, and much more.

Incidentally, it is helpful if the software you have purchased has a facility to save results to *separate* tables and results files. By doing so, if you should miss the occasional match score, the league division tables can be kept up-to-date, independently of results files, by means of a simple editor.

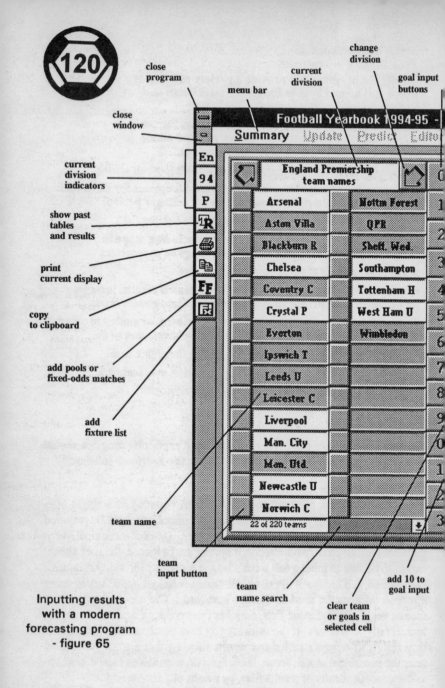

120

close program

close window

menu bar

current division

change division

goal input buttons

current division indicators

show past tables and results

print current display

copy to clipboard

add pools or fixed-odds matches

add fixture list

team name

team input button

team name search

clear team or goals in selected cell

add 10 to goal input

Football Yearbook 1994-95 -

<u>S</u>ummary   Update   Predict   Edito

En
94
P
TR

England Premiership
team names

Arsenal	Nottm Forest
Aston Villa	QPR
Blackburn R	Sheff. Wed.
Chelsea	Southampton
Coventry C	Tottenham H
Crystal P	West Ham U
Everton	Wimbledon
Ipswich T	
Leeds U	
Leicester C	
Liverpool	
Man. City	
Man. Utd.	
Newcastle U	
Norwich C	

22 of 220 teams

0
1
2
3
4
5
6
7
8
9
0
1
2
3

Inputting results
with a modern
forecasting program
- figure 65

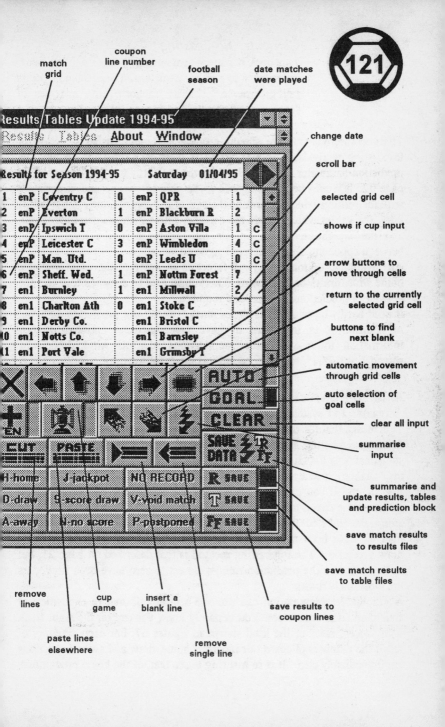

match grid

coupon line number

football season

date matches were played

change date

scroll bar

selected grid cell

shows if cup input

arrow buttons to move through cells

return to the currently selected grid cell

buttons to find next blank

automatic movement through grid cells

auto selection of goal cells

clear all input

summarise input

summarise and update results, tables and prediction block

save match results to results files

save match results to table files

save results to coupon lines

remove lines

cup game

insert a blank line

paste lines elsewhere

remove single line

Results Tables Update 1994-95

Results Tables About Window

Results for Season 1994-95 Saturday 01/04/95

1	enP	Coventry C	0	enP	QPR	1	
2	enP	Everton	1	enP	Blackburn R	2	
3	enP	Ipswich T	0	enP	Aston Villa	1	C
4	enP	Leicester C	3	enP	Wimbledon	4	C
5	enP	Man. Utd.	0	enP	Leeds U	0	C
6	enP	Sheff. Wed.	1	enP	Nottm Forest	7	
7	en1	Burnley	1	en1	Millwall	2	
8	en1	Charlton Ath	0	en1	Stoke C		
9	en1	Derby Co.		en1	Bristol C		
10	en1	Notts Co.		en1	Barnsley		
11	en1	Port Vale		en1	Grimsby T		

AUTO

GOAL

CLEAR

SAVE DATA

EN

CUT PASTE

H-home J-jackpot NO RECORD R SAVE

D-draw S-score draw V-void match T SAVE

A-away N-no score P-postponed PF SAVE

121

Computer Forecasting

This book began by demonstrating that there are many approaches to results prediction. These include points rating systems, such as 'rateform', the analyses of sequences of results and scores, proportions of past match results, dyads, triads, etc.

The software you choose should provide a comprehensive selection of forecasting methods. It is also useful if there is a provision to edit the prediction parameter settings. Consider the 'rateform' method, described on page 12. It would be advantageous to be able to change and experiment with the settings which determine the size of the contributions to the points kitty, the values which decide the category into which the predictions fall, and the 'weighting' which reflects the difference in the level of skill between opponents from different league divisions.

An invaluable option is to *rank* forecasts in order of the most probable home wins, draws or away wins. There must also be a means to select the *number* of predictions of each kind required.

It need hardly be said that facilities must exist to print prediction data, but in addition it is important to have comprehensive options to copy information for use in other applications such as word processors, spreadsheets, DTP programs, communications software, etc.

Analysing Success Rates

A regular and systematic analysis of prediction success rates is crucial. This means that the final scores must be input against each prediction.

A computer listing should show individual successes and failures, while statistical tests (such as chi-square) will measure the overall improvement over chance expectations.

It is helpful if you can rank predictions and then relate the actual match results to the *absolute* rating value for each forecast. To this end a display along the lines of that shown in figure 66 is useful. These particular matches have been ranked from the most probable to the least probable draw prediction. The forecasting method is that described on page 21, but in this instance the prediction ratings closest to zero have been ranked as the most likely draws.

A graphical representation can provide a most informative exposition of your prediction succcesses. You certainly know you are on the right track with success rates of the kind shown in figures 67. For each category of result the numbers of correct or incorrect home, draw and away predictions are immediately clear. It is re-assuring to see that, of the home predictions,

```
RANKED DRAW PREDICTIONS
Match Predictions for Saturday 23/12/95
RESULTS : Draws = 15 (39.47%)   Homes = 16   Aways = 7

Prediction Method... Current Form     ( p=postponed )
```

line	ranking		home team	away team	score	result	correct	rating
34	draw	1	Mansfield T	Hartlepool U	0-3	away		0
20	draw	2	Oldham Ath.	Watford	0-0	draw	yes 1	1
1	draw	3	Ipswich T	Barnsley	2-2	draw	yes 2	1
39	draw	4	Wigan Ath.	Lincoln C	1-1	draw	yes 3	2
22	draw	5	Reading	Wolves	p			-2
28	draw	6	Burnley	Bristol C	0-0	draw	yes 4	-3
18	draw	7	Grimsby T	Leicester C	2-2	draw	yes 5	3
15	draw	8	Wimbledon	Blackburn R	1-1	draw	yes 6	-3
6	draw	9	Coventry C	Everton	2-1	home		-3
25	draw	10	Bournemouth	Hull C	2-0	home		4
8	draw	11	Liverpool	Arsenal	3-1	home		4
7	draw	12	Leeds U	Man. Utd.	3-1	home		-4
38	draw	13	Torquay U	Doncaster R	0-1	away		-5
21	draw	14	Portsmouth	Norwich C	1-0	home		5
33	draw	15	Chester C	Barnet	0-2	away		-6
16	draw	16	Birmingham C	Tranmere R	1-0	home		6
12	draw	17	QPR	Aston Villa	1-0	home		-6
32	draw	18	Bury	Colchester U	0-0	draw	yes 7	7
10	draw	19	Middlesbro	West Ham U	4-2	home		8
42	draw	20	Albion Rov.	Caley Ths	p			-9
40	draw	21	Clydebank	Airdrie	p			9
36	draw	22	Preston NE	Gillingham	0-0	draw	yes 8	9
23	draw	23	Stoke C	Sheff. Utd.	2-2	draw	yes 9	10
9	draw	24	Man. City	Chelsea	0-1	away		11
27	draw	25	Bristol R	Crewe Alex.	1-2	away		-12
17	draw	26	Derby Co.	Sunderland	3-1	home		13
5	draw	27	Leyton O.	Rochdale	2-0	home		13
3	draw	28	Carlisle U	York C	p			13
29	draw	29	Notts Co.	Blackpool	1-1	draw	yes 10	-14
13	draw	30	Sheff. Wed.	Southampton	2-2	draw	yes 11	14
19	draw	31	Luton T	Huddersfield	2-2	draw	yes 12	-15
4	draw	32	Wrexham	Brentford	2-2	draw	yes 13	17
2	draw	33	Brighton	Chesterfield	0-2	away		-17
26	draw	34	Bradford C	Oxford U	1-0	home		18
35	draw	35	Plymouth Arg	Cambridge U	1-0	home		19
11	draw	36	Newcastle U	Nottm Forest	3-1	home		19
37	draw	37	Scarborough	Northampton	2-1	home		-22
30	draw	38	Walsall	Swindon T	0-0	draw	yes 14	-23
41	draw	39	Stirling Alb	Montrose	2-0	home		25
24	draw	40	West Brom	Crystal P	2-3	away		-27
31	draw	41	Wycombe Wan.	Shrewsbury T	2-0	home		-29
14	draw	42	Tottenham H	Bolton Wan.	2-2	draw	yes 15	30

Analysis of home,
draw & away
predictions and
results - figure 67

KEY ....

SHADING
INDICATES
MATCH
RESULT

HOME DRAW AWAY

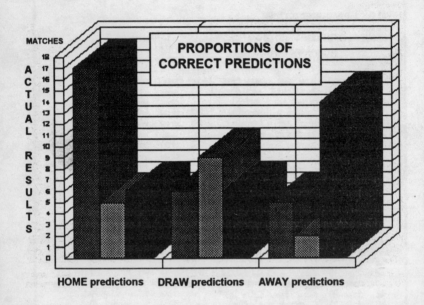

MATCHES

A
C
T
U
A
L

R
E
S
U
L
T
S

18
17
16
15
14
13
12
11
10
9
8
7
6
5
4
3
2
1
0

**PROPORTIONS OF
CORRECT PREDICTIONS**

HOME predictions   DRAW predictions   AWAY predictions

the largest number of match results were indeed home wins. The results for draw and away forecasts show a similarly encouraging distribution of prediction successes.

In figure 68 opposite, you will find another useful graphic, in which the forecasts have been *sorted* in order of **home** ranking. The shading of the vertical bars indicates whether a *result* is a home win, draw or away win, while the height relates to the *prediction ranking* for that particular result. The greater the height the more confident the prediction in the category indicated by the shading.

It can be seen that the top ranked forecasts of each kind have generally been quite successful .... although there are some notable exceptions ! As would be hoped, actual home wins become less frequent from left to right across the page. The lowest ranking home predictions are of course the most likely aways, and the graphic makes it clear that away forecasts are

Analysis of sorted
predictions and results
- figure 68

KEY ....

SHADING
INDICATES
MATCH
RESULT

HOME DRAW AWAY

PREDICTION
RANKING
FOR SHOWN
RESULT

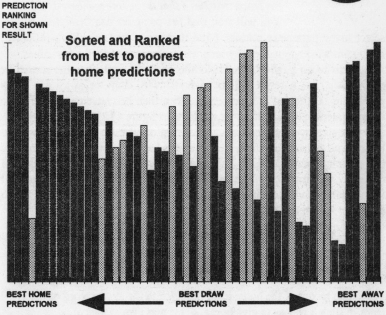

**Sorted and Ranked
from best to poorest
home predictions**

BEST HOME
PREDICTIONS

BEST DRAW
PREDICTIONS

BEST AWAY
PREDICTIONS

particularly succcessful towards the right. As would be hoped, the bulk of
the correct draw predictions are centrally situated in this histogram, that is
between the best of the homes and aways.

COMPUTERISED BETTING ODDS

Betting on soccer results is a growth industry. It is important that the
software you choose should offer features which will help you to beat the
bookie. One useful option is a facility to calculate **'betting odds'**. You can
then use the generated values to make football coupon selections and to
identify the bookmaker's prices which appear to offer the best value.

There follows a step by step guide to compiling betting odds on the
computer. The basic approach was summarised on page 88, and that
section should be read carefully before proceeding with the next.

126

To provide a practical example, calculations have been extracted from the *Yearbook* program (see figure 69 opposite), and the explanation which begins below refers specifically to the odds compiled for the first of the listed matches *(that is the line numbered '1')*.

You will find that the compiler has the option to pre-select many parameter settings (the number of past matches considered, the bookie's over-round, etc) which will influence the final odds values.

As explained on page 88, the basic approach is to calculate the *statistical probability* that a result will be a home win, draw or away win. This probability, expressed as a percentage, can then be converted directly into its equivalent value of odds (see the table in figure 42).

The first step involves determining the past occurrence of wins, draws and losses, and converting these *absolute* numbers to percentages. There are two primary sources of data. The home performance of the home team and the away performance of the away team. For example, consult a football league table and the number of past wins, draws and losses, for two *opposing* teams, might be as follows ...

```
Home Team           vs    Away Team
Home results              Away results
wins  draws  losses       wins  draws  losses
6(hW) 3(hD) 2(hL)         3(aW) 4(aD) 4(aL)
```

The home record of the home team is *added* to the away record of the away team in such a way as to give home, draw and away totals of ...

```
home=(hW+aL)=10    draw=(hD+aD)=7    away=(hL+aW)=5
```

These home, draw and away totals are the first entries in *line 1*, figure 69, and come under the heading *'table.no'* (ie table numbers).

In the next set of figures, the 10 : 7 : 5 ratio has simply been re-stated as percentage values. The heading is *'table-h/d/a%'* (ie table percentages)...

```
home=45.45%  draw=31.82%  away=22.73%
```

These percentages may be regarded as the *probability* of the future occurrence of each result..... subject to a number of refinements, as will now be explained.

In fact there are *two ways* in which the past win, draw and loss record of opposing teams can be utilised. As we have just seen, the data can be extracted directly from the league table. However, to better reflect the 'current form' of each team, a small number of the most recently played matches might also be considered. The precise number of games

Match Odds for Saturday 16/12/95
Algorithm weight.. mean=50% table=20% sequence=30%
User means%.. home=46.0 draw=27.0 away=27.0
Sequence of 5 matches up to (but excluding) 16/12/95
Profit margin set at 110.50%
Draw range adjusted by 90%.

	table.no	table-h/d/a%			seq.no	sequence-h/d/a%		
1...........	10 07 05	45.45	31.82	22.73	07 02 01	70.00	20.00	10.00
2...........	07 09 06	31.82	40.91	27.27	04 04 02	40.00	40.00	20.00
3...........	13 04 05	59.09	18.18	22.73	05 03 02	50.00	30.00	20.00
4...........	16 04 05	64.00	16.00	20.00	07 01 02	70.00	10.00	20.00
5...........	13 06 03	59.09	27.27	13.64	05 04 01	50.00	40.00	10.00
6...........	10 03 06	52.63	15.79	31.58	06 01 03	60.00	10.00	30.00
7...........	08 02 08	44.44	11.11	44.44	04 01 05	40.00	10.00	50.00
8...........	02 06 09	11.76	35.29	52.94	01 04 05	10.00	40.00	50.00

	prob/h%	prob/d%	prob/a%	book/h%	book/d%	book/a%
1.................	53.090	25.864	21.046	57.856	29.709	22.934
2.................	41.364	33.682	24.955	49.851	30.573	30.075
3.................	49.818	26.136	24.045	54.470	29.740	26.291
4.................	56.800	19.700	23.500	57.629	29.028	23.843
5.................	49.818	30.955	19.227	57.887	30.272	22.341
6.................	51.526	19.658	28.816	52.254	29.024	29.223
7.................	43.889	18.722	37.389	44.052	28.920	37.528
8.................	28.353	32.559	39.088	33.654	30.449	46.397

	cp/h%	cp/d%	cp/a%	HOME	home team	DRAW	away team	AWAY	margin
1......	57.895	29.412	23.077	8/11	Arsenal	12/5	Chelsea	10/3	110.384
2......	50.000	30.769	29.412	Evs.	Man. City	9/4	Nottm Forest	12/5	110.181
3......	54.545	29.412	26.316	5/6	QPR	12/5	Bolton Wan.	14/5	110.273
4......	57.895	29.412	23.077	8/11	Huddersfield	12/5	West Brom	10/3	110.384
5......	57.895	30.769	22.222	8/11	Peterborough	9/4	Rotherham U	7/2	110.886
6......	52.381	29.412	29.412	10/11	Hibernian	12/5	Raith Rov.	12/5	111.205
7......	44.444	28.571	38.095	5/4	Hamilton Ac.	5/2	Dumbarton	13/8	111.110
8......	34.783	30.769	45.454	15/8	Queen o' Sth	9/4	Stirling Alb	6/5	111.006

Key...
table.no....................home,draw,away totals taken from current league tables.
table%-h/d/a............home,draw,away percent based on numbers in tables.
seq.no ....home,draw,away totals taken from 'recent' matches played.
sequence%-h/d/a ....home,draw,away percent based on recent result sequences.
prob/(h,d,a)% ....probabilities combining mean, table and sequence data.
book/(h,d,a)%..........probabilities with profit margin included and adjusted range.
cp/(h,d,a)%..............coupon probabilities rounded to traditional betting odds.

comprising the sequence is up to the compiler. In the listed example the last 5 matches played by each team have been selected and (in the same way as before) the home record of the home team is used in conjunction with the away record of the away team.

Referring again to figure 69, under the heading of *'seq.no'* (ie sequence number), the combined 'sequence' totals are ...

```
home=7   draw=2   away=1
```

This **7 : 2 : 1** ratio is represented as percentage values.
The heading is *'sequence-h/d/a%'* (ie sequence percentages)...

```
home=70.00%  draw=20.00%  away=10.00%
```

There are now two sets of probabilities. One is based upon the values taken from the league tables, in which the total number of matches used will increase as the season progresses. The other set of values, a guide to recent form, makes use of a pre-determined sequence of past games.

Remember, the purpose of these calculations is to produce 'betting odds' comparable to those which might be compiled by a professional bookmaker, so in attempting to simulate bookies' prices it is important to *exclude* percentage values which will produce unrealistic values. For example, depending upon the parameter settings and the teams involved, probabilities may vary between as much as 10% and 90%. The danger is that some values, at the extreme limits of this range, will produce exceptionally high or low odds, uncharacteristic of the bookie's coupon.

This problem can be avoided, at least in part, by restricting the *range* of the probabilities. The spread of the percentage values (and consequently the final probabilities and odds) can be constrained by ensuring that they *tend towards* pre-determined levels. These levels can be set by the compiler. The values set here are home=**46.00%**, draw=**27.00%** and away=**27.00%**.

Note that these values are very close to the *true proportions* of home wins, draws and away wins which occur in British league division matches. These pre-set percentage values are referred to as the **'user mean%'**.

It can now be seen that there are *three sets* of figures from which all subsequent probabilities and odds will be derived ...

1. User mean% .... home=46.00   draw=27.00   away=27.00

2. Table% .... home=45.45   draw=31.82   away=22.73

3. Sequence% ...... home=70.00   draw=20.00   away=10.00

The *proportions* in which these values are combined will have considerable bearing upon the final odds. For example increase the weighting of the set **'sequence%'** and recent form becomes more influential .... but with the drawback that unacceptable odds may be introduced. The greater use of **'table%'** data, particularly towards the end of a season, produces less variability. It is also

clear that the larger the contribution of the **'user mean%'** values, the more the final probabilities will stabilize in the direction of the pre-set means.

The user mean%/table%/sequence% ratio is the 'algorithm weight'.

In our example the algorithm weight has been set to... **50 : 20 : 30**.

The comparatively large 50% user mean weighting reduces the range of betting odds, and better reproduces the values which might appear on the professional compiler's coupon. *(The final probabilities will therefore tend towards the pre-set means of home=46%, draw=27% and away=27%).*

By the way, if odds are required which reflect 'true' probabilities (that is leaving aside the bookie's manipulations) then the algorithm weight for the user mean%, and perhaps table%, can be set to zero (a ratio of **0 : 0: 100**).

Having decided upon an algorithm weight of **50 : 20 : 30**, it is a simple matter to combine the three sets of values in the required proportions. The combined set of probabilities for home, draw and away becomes...

Home = ((46.00 X 50) + (45.45 X 20) + (70.00 X 30)) / 100
= (2300 + 909 + 2100) / 100 = **53.090%**

Draw = ((27.00 X 50) + (31.82 X 20) + (20.00 X 30)) / 100
= (1350 + 636.4 + 600) / 100 = **25.864%**

Away = 100 - 53.090 - 25.864   *(ie 100% - home% - draw%)*
= **21.046%**

In figure 69, these three values, which were determined by the algorithm weight, are shown under the column headings *'prob/h%'*, *'prob/d%'* and *'prob/a%'* (ie home win, draw and away win probabilities).

An additional adjustment *might* have been required at this stage. If opposing teams were from different league divisions (*ie cup games*) a change would certainly be needed in the home/draw/away ratio to reflect the variability in skills. Such an adjustment is unnecessary in this example. The next transition comes in two parts.

First of all an adjustment is made which represents the **bookie's over-round**. That is the bookmaker's margin which ensures that he makes a profit. In the on-going example the over-round was set to a typical **10.5%**. It is therefore necessary to increase *each* probability by this amount.

The revised values are...

Home = (53.090 X 110.5) / 100 = **58.664%**

Draw = (25.864 X 110.5) / 100 = **28.580%**

Away = 110.5 - 58.664 - 28.58 = **23.256%**

There is another adjustment. The range of draw odds offered by a bookmaker is small; very much smaller than those for homes and aways. **Consequently it is necessary to introduce an option to *further restrict* the spread of the draw probability.** This is achieved by moving the value *towards* the over-rounded *user mean%* for draws. You will recall that the pre-set user mean for draws in our example was **27%**.

First of all the *over-rounded user mean%* must be calculated...

Over-rounded draw mean = (27.00 X 110.5) / 100 = **29.835%**

The computer user now has the option to move the value of the previously calculated draw probability, which was **28.580%**, in the direction of the over-rounded user mean, of **29.835%**. (*In this case the difference between the two values is not large, but this will not always be so*).

The *degree of adjustment* of this difference is yet another parameter set by the software user. Any value up to, and including, 100% could be selected. Of course, if 100% were chosen, the derived draw probability would take the same value as the over-rounded draw mean (ie 29.835%).

In our example it has been decided to adjust the difference in the draw probability by a factor of **90%**. Remember, the greater the adjustment the more the final draw probability will tend towards the over-rounded pre-set draw mean. In this example the *difference* between the over-rounded draw mean and the previously calculated draw probability is as follows...

Difference in probabilities = 29.835% less 28.580% = **1.255%**

Note that in this case the result is positive, but, depending upon the relative size of the two draw percentage values, it could be negative.

Now *reduce* this difference of **1.255** to **90%** and *multiply* by **-1**....

Draw Range Adjustment = ((1.255 X 90) / 100)) X -1 = **-1.1295%**

(*The need to multiply by -1 will soon become clear*).

Now subtract the *draw range adjustment* from the previously calculated *draw probability* to get the revised value for a draw...

Draw = 28.58 - (-1.1295)

= 28.58 + 1.1295 = **29.7095%**

Observe that the revised draw probability has moved *closer* to the over-rounded mean draw value set by the user. The new value is shown in figure 69, in the column headed *'book/d%'* (bookie's draw percentage).

The change in the draw probability in this example was only 1.1295%, but whatever the value, the *totalled* probabilities for home win, draw and away win must remain at 110.5%. **Any change in the draw probablity must always be *passed* to the home and away probabilities to achieve a total equal to the bookie's margin.**

The over-rounded home and away probabilities have been calculated as 58.664% and 23.256% respectively. The draw range adjustment was calculated as -1.1295%. This amount is passed *proportionately* to the home and away percentages. The proportion of the -1.1295% passed to the home probability is calculated as follows...

Home adjustment = (58.664 / (58.664 + 23.256)) X -1.1295

= (58.664 / 81.92) X -1.1295 = -0.8088

The home probability then becomes...

Home = 58.664 + (-0.8088) = 57.856%

The away probability becomes...

Away = 110.5 - 57.856 - 29.7095 *(ie 110.5% - home% - draw%)*

= 22.934%

Note that the home, draw and away probabilities total 110.5%, and that a slight *increase* in the value of the draw has given rise to an equivalent *fall* in the combined values for the home win and away win.

The new probabilties for *match '1'* are now...

home=57.856% draw=29.709% away=22.934%

These are the values shown in figure 69 under the headings *'book/h%'*, *'book/d%'*, and *'book/a%'* (ie bookie's home, draw and away percentage).

The final step is to *convert* the calculated probabilities to the 'traditional' values of **betting odds** found on the bookmakers' coupons. Unfortunately few probabilities are likely to convert directly into those values of odds which are commonly used by bookmakers in the United Kingdom.

It is necessary to compare the calculated probabilities with those contained in an array of probabilities and betting odds (of the kind shown in the table in figure 42), and then to select those odds which are represented by the probabilities *closest* to the required values. The process is further

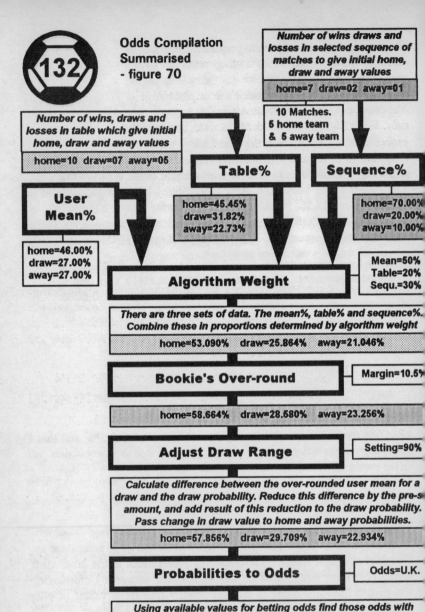

132

Odds Compilation
Summarised
- figure 70

Number of wins draws and
losses in selected sequence of
matches to give initial home,
draw and away values

home=7 draw=02 away=01

10 Matches.
5 home team
& 5 away team

Number of wins, draws and
losses in table which give initial
home, draw and away values

home=10 draw=07 away=05

Table%

home=45.45%
draw=31.82%
away=22.73%

Sequence%

home=70.00%
draw=20.00%
away=10.00%

**User
Mean%**

home=46.00%
draw=27.00%
away=27.00%

Algorithm Weight

Mean=50%
Table=20%
Sequ.=30%

*There are three sets of data. The mean%, table% and sequence%.
Combine these in proportions determined by algorithm weight*

home=53.090%   draw=25.864%   away=21.046%

Bookie's Over-round

Margin=10.5%

home=58.664%   draw=28.680%   away=23.256%

Adjust Draw Range

Setting=90%

*Calculate difference between the over-rounded user mean for a
draw and the draw probability. Reduce this difference by the pre-s
amount, and add result of this reduction to the draw probability.
Pass change in draw value to home and away probabilities.*

home=57.856%   draw=29.709%   away=22.934%

Probabilities to Odds

Odds=U.K.

*Using available values for betting odds find those odds with
probability percentages closest to the calculated values*

home=57.895%   draw=29.412%   away=23.077%

FINAL ODDS... HOME 8/11   DRAW 12/5   AWAY 10/3

complicated by the need to retain a percentage total, as far as practicable, equal to the bookie's profit margin.

In the current example, up to this stage, the draw probability has been calculated as 29.709%. The traditional odds *probability* closest to this value (using the table in figure 42) is 29.412%. **The draw odds represented by this probability are 12/5**.

It is now necessary to calculate the *difference* between the final draw probability and the *previously calculated* draw percentage ...

Change in draw probability = 29.412 - 29.709 = -0.297%

The next step is to *add* this 'change' to the last calculated probability for an away win. This produces a *revised* probability for the **away** ...

Revised away probability = 22.934 + (-0.297) = 22.637%

The best available betting odds can now be found for this adjusted away percentage. Again using figure 42, it can be seen that the closest value to 22.637% is 23.077%. **The corresponding betting odds are 10/3**.

Last of all work out the *revised* **home** probability using the final draw and away values which have just been calculated ...

Revised home probability = 110.5 - 29.412 - 23.077 = 58.011%

As before, there are no betting odds which correspond precisely to this value. The nearest percentage is 57.895%. **The odds are 8/11**.

The final probabilities for *match '1'* are...

```
home=57.895%  draw=29.412%  away=23.077%
```

These are the values shown in figure 69 under the headings *'cp/h%'*, *'cp/d%'*, and *'cp/a%'* (ie final 'coupon' home, draw and away percentages). These probabilities correspond to betting odds of...

```
HOME 8/11   DRAW 12/5   AWAY 10/3
```

Note that the *sum* of the final percentage values is 110.384% (see the column headed *'margin'* in figure 69). The final value has drifted a little away from the pre-set margin of 110.5%, but the change is negligible.

A useful option in the *Yearbook* software is to show 'odds' as *decimal values*, which are widely used elsewhere in Europe. Such a representation is undoubtedly superior to that favoured in U.K. betting shops, and requires less manipulation of the figures in the last stages of the odds algorithm. The decimal system produces summed probabilities much closer to the pre-set bookie's margin.

134

The compilation process is admittedly elaborate, but this is just the sort of thing a computer does best !

A step by step summary is provided in figure 70. In particular note that the following parameters settings are under the direct control of the software user...

Algorithm Weight...........*ratio of user mean%/table%/sequence%*
User Mean%....................*pre-set home, draw and away probabilities*
Sequence of matches.......*number of matches to be used in analysis*
Bookies Profit Margin....*the over-round setting; any value up to 50%*
Draw Range Setting........*degree of adjustment to draw probability*
Odds Representation......*selection of U.K. or 'decimal' odds*

It has just been demonstrated that these settings may be selected with the specific purpose of reproducing bookie's odds. Alternatively the parameters can be chosen in such a way as to calculate the 'true' probabilty (and so display the 'fair' odds) for each result.

It is not being suggested for a moment that the use of computer generated values will make the professional compiler redundant. There are many factors which it would be difficult or impossible to quantify for use in a computer system, and it is not unknown for bookmakers to shorten or lengthen odds in response to anticipated levels of backing. However you will discover that a computer can generate a list of match odds remarkably similar to those found on the fixed-odds football coupon.

ELECTRONIC MAIL

The time will soon come when you will begin to feel left behind if you have not been 'connected' to the Internet. The Net and the associated technologies change almost daily, however one excellent provision, which has been around for several years now, is to send data or program files attached to e-mail messages. This is of particular interest to the user of soccer software, who perhaps has not the time, opportunity or inclination, to update a database of match scores on a regular basis. For such a person, the weekly supply of a set of data files, which includes up-to-date results and tables, can be a godsend. The supplier of your soccer or forecasting software should be able to provide such a service at a minimal cost, probably only a few pence per week.

The mail-reader which comes with your communications software will recognise the encoded data file attached to an e-mail message. It then drops the file into a designated download directory on your computer system.

It is evident that, when you select an Internet 'provider', software which ensures error free file transfer should be high on your list of priorities.

WORLD WIDE WEB

There are millions of addresses on the World Wide Web and both soccer and gambling are well represented. The sites are continually evolving and a few of those listed below may have disappeared. Others will of course have been added. Nevertheless there is sure to be more than enough here to get you started and most pages contain links to other useful destinations. All of the URL's (*site locations*) have the same prefix (**http://**), so this has been omitted from the list.....

Soccer and Gambling Search Index.... *The Sites listed below - plus more !*
members.aol.com/sitelist/master.html

The Soccer Form Book.... *A Must For The Serious Soccer Punter*
www.formbook.com/

Virtual Library.... *Lists Many Soccer Pages on the Web*
www.atm.ch.cam.ac.uk/sports/webs.html

Yahoo Soccer.... *The Yahoo Search Engine for Soccer*
www.yahoo.com/Recreation/Sports/Soccer/

RSSSF Archive.... *Everything you need to know on World Soccer*
info.risc.uni-linz.ac.at:70/1/misc-info/rsssf/archive.html

Association of Soccer Statisticians.... *All Sorts of Data for the Enthusiast*
www.innotts.co.uk/~soccerstats/

In the back of the Net.... *Soccer on the Internet*
www.mcewans.co.uk/football/rep_misc.htm

The Sports Server.... *Reuters Information Service*
www2.nando.net/newsroom/sports/oth/1995/oth/soc/ feat/soc.html

SoccerNews Online.... *World Soccer Headquarters !*
www.csn.net/~eid/soccer/sccrindx.html

Soccernet.... *Includes Results For England and Scotland*
www.soccernet.com/

FIFA.... *Official Page*   **UEFA....** *Official Page*
www.fifa.com   **www.uefa.org**

SMARTsig.... *Statistical and Systematic Approach To Betting*
www.dircon.co.uk/smartsig

Intertops.... *Online Soccer Betting*
www.intertops.co.at/inter/engl/more.html

Eurototo.... *Soccer Betting on the Internet*
206.31.72.146

WWW Toto.... *Make Predictions on the 'Toto'*
www.astro.uva.nl/michielb/toto/toto.html

Socrates.... *UK Soccer Ratings for Results Prediction*
members.aol.com/soccerslot/socrates.html

Mabel's Tables.... *UK Soccer Tables and Results*
members.aol.com/mabstabs/soccer.html

The12Xpert.... *Some Help to 'Beat The Bookie'*
members.aol.com/the12Xpert/soccer.html

Forth Dimension.... *Soccer Software, Statistics, Pools, Fixed-Odds*
users.aol.com/soccerslot/forthdim.html

Pools Check.... *Sponsored by Zetters Pools*
www.soccernet.com/soccfile/results/zetsplus.html

The Half Decent Web Site.... *Alternative Culture 'Magazine'*
www.wsc.co.uk/wsc/

Aussie Forecast.... *Aussie Soccer and Download Free Software*
users.aol.com/fdandco/ausff.html

European Forecast.... *Software for 32 European Leagues and Download*
users.aol.com/fdandco/eurff.html

Net resources and places to begin a search on the Web on *any* subject.....

Yahoo.... **www.yahoo.com**

Lycos Database.... **lycos.cs.cmu.edu/**

Starting Point.... **www.stpt.com/**

Yellow Pages.... **www.mcp.com**

LinkStar.... **www.linkstar.com**

InfoSeek.... **www.infoseek.com**

Net Resources.... **www.eit.com/web/web.html**

Commercial Sites on The Net.... **www.directory.net/**

DejaNews.... **www.dejanews.com/**

Global Network Navigator.... **www.gnn.com/gnn/index.html**

Harvest.... **harvest.cs.colorado.edu/**

Today's Cool Site.... **www.infi.net/cool.html**

Information Bank.... **www.clark.net/pub/global/front.html**

Yanoff's List.... **www.uwm.edu/Mirror/inet.services.html**

MCNY Links.... **www.mcny.com/linkspage/**

The WWW Virtual Library.... *Wide Ranging General Subject Catalogue*
www.w3.org/hypertext/DataSources/bySubject/Overview.

A 'PERMUTATION' PROGRAM

There follows a description of a computer program written in the BASIC language for IBM compatible Personal Computers using DOS.

The program generates 'permutations'. To develop and modify program code it is of course necessary that you have some understanding of programming.

The program listed below can be run only if you have suitable programming software. A compiled BASIC is preferred. The chosen compiler is *PowerBASIC*, although the use of any version of BASIC should necessitate only minor changes to the listed code.

As you examine the code you will notice that there are no line numbers. These are less often used in programming nowadays. They tend to encourage undisciplined use of the GOTO command and generally clutter up a program making it harder to understand. The *procedures* and *functions* used here make it easier to visualise the flow of execution and, once created, modules can often be extracted in their entirety for use within other programs.

The program is written in text mode with a screen of 25 rows and 80 columns. To reduce the volume of code to manageable proportions, error checking and the verification of input, has been omitted. Consequently, when running this program, it is advisable to enter data as instructed, and within sensible numerical limits.

The program begins with the statement DEFINT a-y. This means that, by default, every variable with a name beginning *a* through to y (case being insignificant) represents an integer value. It then becomes necessary to identify only the non-integer types as they are used.

The physical location of individual procedures and functions within the listed code is, in terms of compilation at least, immaterial. In fact modules are located *before* the main control structure. That is they are listed ahead of that body of code which dictates overall flow.

It is has been said that the program provides 'permutations'. However, in practice, it should be noted that the gambler's permutation is the statistician's *combination*. For the purposes of this program the terms permutation and combination are interchangeable. But remember, the algorithm reproduced here is that for what is correctly known as the combination.

The listed code can be incorporated in other applications which make use of permutations. For example, it might be used to provide 'perms' of lottery numbers, for pools coupon selections, or in fixed-odds calculations.

As it stands the code permutes consecutive numbers beginning from '1'.

You must develop the program to accept the input of individual match or lottery numbers.
This is typical of the screen output ....

```
Input the total number of
selections ( max 20 ) - ?   6
Input the number of matches
you wish to perm - ?   4
4 from 6 gives 15 combinations
The combinations are -
         1   2   3   4
         1   2   3   5
         1   2   3   6
         1   2   4   5
         1   2   4   6
         1   2   5   6
         1   3   4   5
         1   3   4   6
         1   3   5   6
         1   4   5   6
         2   3   4   5
         2   3   4   6
         2   3   5   6
         2   4   5   6
         3   4   5   6
Press any key
```

The program begins by defining all 'A-Y' variables as integers.
An array is dimensioned. In this case the total number of selections is limited to 20, as in 'perm x from 20'. The screen is set up for display of black background and white text and then cleared. The main body of the program prompts for input of the total number of selections, then the number of lines (matches) to perm. It uses three program modules.

```
DEFINT A-Y
DIM A(1:20)
SCREEN 0
COLOR 7,0
CLS
```

The Factorial function ...
This function calculates factorials, which in turn are used in the formula which calculates the total number of combinations. For example 4 factorial is written as 4! and is equal to $1 \times 2 \times 3 \times 4 = 24$.

```
DEF FNFactorial#(pnumber)
  LOCAL fcount, zfnumber#

    zfnumber# = 1
    FOR fcount = pnumber TO 2 STEP -1
        zfnumber# = zfnumber# * fcount
    NEXT fcount

    FNFactorial# = zfnumber#

END DEF
```

The Perm function ...
This next function calculates the TOTAL number of combinations by using the factorial function just listed. For example given 'perm 4 from 6' the value '4' is represented by the identifier 'pselect', and '6' by 'total'. In this case the function would return '15'.

```
DEF FNCalcPerms%(total,pselect)

    LOCAL diff, perm, zftotal#, zfselect#, zfdiff#

    perm = zftotal#:      diff  =  total - pselect
    zftotal#   =  FNFactorial#(total)
    zfselect#  =  FNFactorial#(pselect)
    zfdiff#    =  FNFactorial#(diff)
    perm = zftotal# / (zfselect# * zfdiff#)

    FNCalcPerms%  =   perm

END DEF
```

The Combinations procedure ...
This is the main module which actually lists all combinations. Using the example 'perm 4 from 6' the identifier 'selections'='6' and 'matches'='4'. The value 'totcombinations' has already been calculated using the perm function above. The variable 'countcombinations' is used to end the listing of combinations within the loop when it equals 'totcombinations'.
The identifier 'firstentry' initially equals zero, and ensures certain operations are carried out when the routine is first called. For example the array values of A() are set to zero and other variable values are initiated. The combinations are listed to the screen.

```
SUB CalcCombinations

SHARED selections, matches, firstentry, A(), totcombinations
LOCAL x, y, z, count, countcombinations

    firstentry=0
    DO
    IF firstentry = 0 THEN
            x = 0: y = matches: firstentry = 1:
            ERASE A: countcombinations = 0:
    ELSE
            FOR y = 1 TO matches
                    x = A(matches+1-y)
                     IF x<>selections+1-y THEN EXIT FOR
            NEXT y
    END IF
    FOR z = 1 TO y
            A(matches+z-y) = x + z
    NEXT z

    INCR countcombinations
    FOR count=1 TO matches: PRINT A(count);: NEXT count
    PRINT
    LOOP UNTIL countcombinations=totcombinations

END SUB
```

*The **MAIN** body of the program
which first prompts for input of
the total number of selections, then
the number of lines (matches) to
be permuted ....*

```
PRINT " Input the total number of selections ( max 20 ) - ";
INPUT selections
PRINT " Input the number of matches you wish to perm - ";
INPUT matches
```

The total combinations are calculated ....

```
totcombinations=FNCalcPerms(selections,matches)
PRINT matches; "from"; selections; "gives";
totcombinations; "combinations"
```

The sub-routine 'CalcCombinations' is called which lists the perms ...

```
PRINT " Combinations are -"
CALL CalcCombinations
```

Press any key to exit program .....

```
PRINT " Press any key";
WHILE INKEY$ = "": WEND

END
```

Forth Dimension
28 Macbeth Road
Dunfermline.
KY11 4EG

*It is clearly not practical to include the program code
for a complete forecasting system. However if you have
compact, self-contained code, which might interest the
readers of future editions of Football Fortunes, do
please send it along to 'Forth Dimension'. In fact any queries or
comments, on any relevant subject, are most welcome.*

Football Yearbook – Computer Software

The *Windows™* **FOOTBALL YEARBOOK** is computer software which will appeal both to the soccer enthusiast and to those with an interest in football results forecasting. The program requires a personal computer with a VGA display, 3mb of RAM, and a minimum of a 386SX processor.

The program takes the form of a computerised football annual.

It comes with full results and tables for the English Premier League, Football League and Scottish Football League, since 1987.

There are many text and graphics displays, with all the printing, clipboard, copying and saving operations associated with a top *Windows* program.

The input of match results for the current season is easy. The user can then analyse the performance of each and every team as the season progresses.

The *Football Yearbook* is chock-a-block with statistics.

The software was developed from the popular *Football Forecast* for DOS and includes both old and new forecasting methods. The *Yearbook* will predict home, draw and away results for league and cup matches between teams from the major league divisions, plus the four minor tables found on pools and fixed-odds coupons. There is no limit to the number of predictions which may be made. Forecasts can be sorted, copied and printed, just as required. Prediction success rates can be analysed.

Forecasting methods make use of the data from results and table files. Forecasts take into consideration selected sequences of matches, goal averages, goals scored, and many other factors. In fact the user selects from a range of forecasting criteria and sets the prediction parameters. This means that there is complete freedom to amend and test the predictive algorithms and formulae.

Also included in the *Yearbook* is a unique and extensive feature which generates football betting odds. Odds can be compiled in such a way as to simulate those found on the bookmaker's fixed-odds coupons, or used simply as a forecasting tool to aid betting selections.

The odds are based upon accurately compiled statistical probabilities, and the formulae and parameters can be accessed and edited by the user.

A comprehensive instructional handbook accompanies the software, which is despatched with up-to-date results and tables for the current season.

Payment may be made by cheque, postal order or credit card. The *Yearbook* is offered to readers of *Football Fortunes* at a total cost of £17.00.

Ask for details concerning the availability of fixture lists, results and tables for the whole 20th century, and regular e-mail data updates if required.

Forth Dimension, 28 Macbeth Road,
Dunfermline, Fife, Scotland. KY11 4EG

Contact : **Bill Hunter**   Tel. or Fax : **01383 721729**
E-mail : Soccerslot@aol.com
http://users.aol.com/soccerslot/forthdim.html

FORTH

D I M E N S I O N

AVAILABLE FROM SEPTEMBER 1996

FOOTBALL FORECAST

Software providing football match prediction and analysis has become increasingly popular for home use and office syndicate. 'Football Forecast' is undoubtedly the best program of its kind for PC's using DOS. This program forecasts draws, homes, aways and scores for league and cup matches between football teams from all divisions currently found on 'pools' and bookmakers' coupons. Odds are estimated for every

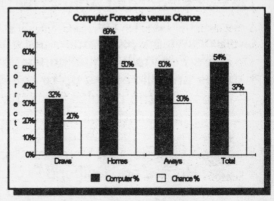

possible result and the 'form' of each team is analysed.
Many variables are considered in assessing comparative team strengths which can be 'weighted' at a level set by the user. The update of match results is simple and rapid. Relegations, promotions and new teams can be entered. The forecasting and statistical data are accessible for printing. Comprehensive statistical analyses are provided and there is an exceptional 'Facts and Figures' component. The special price of £12.95, to purchasers of 'Football Fortunes', represents a saving of £10.00 over that which has been advertised in national magazines and newspapers. The complete DOS package, consists of ....

The Up-to-Date UK prediction program
AUSSIE Forecast for the summer season
'LinePlan' software to check pools plans
The 'European' version for 32 countries
A sixty page instructional handbook

*Contact **Bill Hunter** at ...*

FORTH DIMENSION, 28 Macbeth Road
Dunfermline, Fife, Scotland. KY11 4EG

FOOTBALL FANS

Dr Fox's Football Annual for DOS lets you use your computer to keep track of your team and spot likely draws on your pools coupon.

Dr Fox's Football Annual contains all the season's fixtures and all results up to the date of dispatch, as well as all the results from the last five seasons. It's got more statistics than John Motson !

Covers the Premier League, Endsleigh League, Scottish League, GM Vauxhall Conference and ICIS, Beazer Homes and Unibond Premier Divisions.

It is very easy to use and lets you analyse results in many different ways.

For users of *Forth Dimension's* Football Yearbook the price of the annual is only £7.99.

It comes complete with FIXTURE LISTS which can be used within the Yearbook program.

Send your name and address, quoting your Yearbook *registration reference*, along with a cheque or PO, made payable to Dr. Fox, to the address below ....

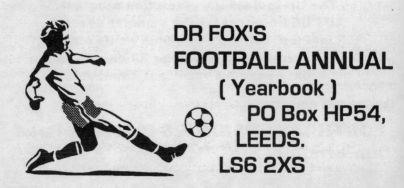

DR FOX'S
FOOTBALL ANNUAL
(Yearbook)
PO Box HP54,
LEEDS.
LS6 2XS

Systems Methodologies And Rational Thinking

.... special interest group

The UKs only systems + statistics magazine

The idea for the **SMART** special interest group was born out of the enthusiasm and passion of a dedicated band of individuals who enjoy making profits from a statistical and structured approach to their betting. Because of the advances that can be achieved through discussion and the sharing and pooling of ideas, it was decided to offer membership of the group to a much wider audience.

What are the aims of SMART ?

We were established to build a network of intelligent, rational thinking individuals and groups who know that profitable betting strategies can be achieved through careful planning and observation. Using the benefits of shared information and knowledge, distributed through the monthly magazine, the group intends to help all members to establish how, where and when the odds are in favour of the bettor, and how to find 'value'. Equally important of course is to show where and when research has shown that betting opportunities are worthwhile, or where odds are grossly out of line with what should be expected.

All forms of intelligent betting are covered, without limits, the magazine content is in fact based entirely upon contributions from the members themselves and everyone is encouraged to participate. The subjects covered therefore reflect what our members themselves want, and not what somebody this end thinks they want. Currently around 60% is horseracing, 20% soccer (during the season) and the remainder is taken with whatever is the current topic of conversation, staking or money management, spread betting, other sports betting, book and computer product reviews, etc. etc.

Our motto is - DON'T GAMBLE - INVEST!

Established in 1994 the group has grown steadily in size and is now distributed to well over a dozen countries world-wide. Members range from enthusiastic amateurs to professionals, members who do not bet to people who make their living from betting, from teenagers to octogenarians, university professors to retired manual workers and each complementing the other with their common purpose.

We give you the truth behind commercial computer horseracing software with our on-going computer challenge. Discounts on many big name products from Raceform, Racing Post, Association of Football Statisticians to name but a few. Free horseracing software, big discounts on other computer products and books for both horses and soccer.

Further details (in strict confidence) by sending a 1st class stamp to ....

SMARTsig (FF), PO Box 29, Mansfield. NG19 8UA

Tel. or fax... 01623 812400   E-mail... smartsig@dircon.co.uk

Look up the SMART Web site at... http://www.dircon.co.uk/smartsig

The Windows Fixed-Odds Calculator

is designed for use with the bookie's fixed-odds football coupon. The software provides invaluable betting and pay-out data for varying levels of stake and values of odds.

Selections				Stake	Date
07	New	Insert	Exit	00 — 10	20/12/94
◆	Clear	Add	Delete		

	Line	Team	Predict	Odds	Input	
▨	12	Tottenham	home	6/5	☒	C /
▨	20	Wolves	away	9/4	☒	
▨	25	Sunderland	home	13/8	☒	0 1
▨	37	Exeter	draw	12/5	☒	
▨	39	Rochdale	home	8/13	☒	2 3
▪	47	Dundee	home	2/1	☒	
▪	57	Arbroath	away	6/4	☒	4 5
▪					☐	6 7
▪					☐	
▪					☐	8 9

☐ Single(s)
☐ Double(s)
☐ Treble(s)
☐ 4 fold(s)
☒ 5 fold(s) 21
☒ 6 fold(s) 7
☒ 7 fold(s) 1
☐ 8 fold(s)
☐ 9 fold(s)

☐ 10 fold(s)
☐ 11 fold(s)
☐ 12 fold

Correct [x]	7 of 7
Win Perms	29
Tot. Perms	29
Cost of Bet	2.90

Display

Bet	Pay
Odds	Margin
Copy	Print
Mini	Info

Tax ● No ○ pre-paid ○ post-paid

It is a simple matter to prepare a bet and to experiment with different permutations, selections and prices. Use the calculator to achieve an acceptable balance of cost and return, and to check your winnings. The Fixed-Odds calculator requires Windows 3.1 or 95 with a minimum of a 386SX processor. Typical displays are shown below. All calculator displays may be printed or copied to the 'clipboard'.

```
PAYOUT 23/5/96

  5 of 5 correct
  13/5 9/4 7/4
  13/8 12/5

Treble(s)  = 10
 Pays £30.1843
4 fold(s)  =  5
 Pays £46.6402
5 fold(s)  =  1
 Pays £28.7162

Total £105.5407
( tax pre-paid )
```

```
BET for 23/5/96

  1  Sheffield    away
  4  Nott.For.    draw
 31  Colchester   away
 47  Dundee       away
 53  East Fife    draw

 Treble(s)  = 10
 4 fold(s)  =  5
 5 fold(s)  =  1
 Total Bet Lines = 16

 Cost £1.76
 at £00.10 per unit.
 ( includes 10% tax )
```

The package includes 3.5" diskette with installation and running instructions. Total payment .... by credit card, cheque, postal order or cash ...... only £3.50

ADVERTISERS and USER GROUPS

If you wish to include an advertisement,
or other information, in future editions of
Football Fortunes then contact ..

Forth Dimension
Attn. Bill Hunter
28 Macbeth Road, Dunfermline, Fife,
Scotland. KY11 4EG

Tel/Fax : 01383 721729
E-mail : Soccerslot@aol.com

READERS' CONTRIBUTIONS

There can be little doubt that new material will
be gathered for inclusion in future publications
and amendments made to the current edition !
Your contributions or comments are therefore
most welcome and should be forwarded to
Bill Hunter at the above address.